T0209936

How the Bible Defines:
Election

Clearing the Muddied Waters of Calvinism

Caleb Bulow

WESTBOW
PRESS®
A DIVISION OF THOMAS NELSON
& ZONDERVAN

This book is a work of non-fiction. Unless otherwise noted, the author and the publisher make no explicit guarantees as to the accuracy of the information contained in this book and in some cases, names of people and places have been altered to protect their privacy.

WestBow Press books may be ordered through booksellers or by contacting:

WestBow Press
A Division of Thomas Nelson & Zondervan
1663 Liberty Drive
Bloomington, IN 47403
www.westbowpress.com
1 (866) 928-1240

Because of the dynamic nature of the Internet, any web addresses or links contained in this book may have changed since publication and may no longer be valid. The views expressed in this work are solely those of the author and do not necessarily reflect the views of the publisher, and the publisher hereby disclaims any responsibility for them.

Unless otherwise stated, scripture quotations are taken from the New King James Version®. Copyright © 1982 by Thomas Nelson. Used by permission. All rights reserved.

ISBN: 978-1-9736-3984-8 (sc)
ISBN: 978-1-9736-3986-2 (hc)
ISBN: 978-1-9736-3985-5 (e)

Library of Congress Control Number: 2018910974

Print information available on the last page.

WestBow Press rev. date: 10/09/2018

CONTENTS

PREFACE

In theological circles, the doctrine of Election is undoubtedly one of the major battlegrounds of debate where many scholars and students have fiercely fought. The battles have been so numerous and heated that the mere mention of the word "election" can cause a person's inner defenses to rise. But do we really understand what the Biblical word "election" means? The Greek lexicons give us definitions of the underlying words, but what would a full Biblical word study reveal? This book contains just such a study, presented in a way that any English-speaking Bible student can understand.

Looking back through time, I remember studying the Bible in my late teens and somehow getting the idea that "elect" could often be translated as "choice." Not choice in the sense of making a selection, but choice in the sense of prized and special. I don't recall what put this idea in my head, but at the time I was convinced it came from the Lord. Of course, I went to all the passages containing the word "elect" in the New Testament and substituted "choice" to see if it fit the flow of context. To my delight, I found that it did. That was adequate confirmation for me and from that day forward I was convinced that the definition was correct. Finding that others didn't readily adopt the idea did little to shake my confidence. However, an in-depth discussion with a good friend on reformed theology forced me to carefully reevaluate my thinking.

Prior to the conversation with my friend, I discovered a

resource that enabled me (with minimal Greek background) to identify occurrences of Greek New Testament words in the Septuagint (an ancient Greek translation of the Old Testament). This was a thrilling find, for it increased the number of contexts available to me when I did word studies of relatively obscure New Testament words. I found the Old Testament narrative type contexts helped me understand how the words were used in everyday life.

One of the first words I looked up was "propitiation." Did you know that a form of this word appears in the story of Jacob's fearful preparation to meet Esau? The gifts that Jacob sent to his brother were meant to "appease" Esau, and the word "appease" is a form of propitiate. Meditating on that passage proved a great help in understanding the concept of propitiation.

As might be expected in the discussion with my friend, the topic of election eventually came up. Not surprisingly, my friend was not receptive to the definition of "choice" for "elect." It occurred to me that my Septuagint resource could be used to verify my claim regarding the definition of the Greek word for election. To my surprise, when I looked up the words for elect in the Septuagint, I found an almost overwhelming amount of material to sift through and examine.

The intent of this booklet is to share what I learned regarding the three Greek forms of the word "elect." Please be aware that it is not my intent to tackle within these pages all the topics and doctrines related to election, such as the sovereignty of God, foreknowledge, free will, predestination, and etc. The discussion herein will be restricted to the definitions of three Greek words translated as "chose," "elect," and "election."

Some will likely say that I am redefining these words to fit my own preconceived notions, but I think this is not the case. My method of word study was not based on questionable procedures such as etymology or alternative definitions. It was based, as you can see, on looking at each context where the words were used, which is the recommended method for discovering the meaning of a word. Furthermore, I found that my preconceived notions changed as I went through the study, which is surely an indication that I was not fixed on my idea. Finally, the definitions derived herein are not entirely new but can be found in good lexicons and dictionaries.

Others may claim that the conclusions presented herein make certain Scriptures more difficult to understand. But I think this is because we are accustomed to looking at these passages in a particular way and it's difficult to un-learn what we thought we knew.

As I've gone through this study, I have endeavored to keep in mind that I want to learn the truth. It's of no benefit to hold on to false doctrines, for the truth is true, and my beliefs do not change reality. Therefore, it behooves me to lay aside my own ideas and seek out the truth. I encourage the reader to be of this mind and search for the truth, for God is truth. To Him be the glory.

1

BACKGROUND

Navigating the Original Languages

Cainan took a long look out over the fertile plains, pausing from his labor for just a brief minute. It was amazing how far one could see when one was elevated a mere hundred feet or so. Looking down the side of the brick and mortar structure from where he was sitting, he marveled again at what men could do when they set their minds to a common task. It was said that the goal of this tower was to reach up to heaven, and he did not doubt that it would achieve the goal. Lost in his thoughts, he did not notice anyone approaching until the voice of Diklah, his supervisor, penetrated his thoughts from only a short distance behind him. Guiltily, Cainan hurriedly started to his feet. Judging from the tone of his voice, Diklah was not in a good mood. As he turned, he saw his supervisor looking questioningly at him, as if waiting for an answer.

"What was that, sir?" he asked as he began edging his way around Diklah.

"Haben Sie Felsen in den Mund?," growled Diklah as he moved closer, "Stoppen Sie Ihr Gesicht, wenn Sie mit mir sprechen und sich wieder an die Arbeit!"

Hurriedly, Cainan scampered by Diklah, saying quickly, "I just stopped for a second to grab a breath of fresh air, sir. It sure is nice up here, isn't it, sir? Nice talking to you, I'll be back to work now. See you later, sir."

"I wonder what weed he is smoking now?" thought Cainan as he bounded up a flight of stairs, "He sounded a lot more garbled than usual – must be some powerful stuff."

Arriving at the top of the stairs, he saw his co-worker, Seba, already back at work. Hearing him arrive, Seba turned and said, "Tutaj jesteś! Chodź tu i pomóż mi z tym."

"What was that?" said Cainan as he headed over to grab his tool belt. Not hearing any response, Cainan glanced back to see Seba gaping at him. "What's the matter with you? You look like you've seen a ghost."

Seba scowled, "Grasz jakiś żart na mnie? Co się dzieje?"

It was Cainan's turn to stare, "Seba, that didn't make any sense. You sounded worse than Diklah! What's gotten into you guys?"

~ ~ ~   ~ ~ ~   ~ ~ ~

"And that's where it all started," thought Lucius as he set down his pen. Ever since that day, men have struggled to communicate between various groups of people, trying to overcome the language barriers which had been put in place by God. There was a lot of progress in the last hundred years or so, after Alexander the Great conquered most of the world. The Greek language had spread until it was spoken by nearly everyone throughout all the civilized regions. Even *he* spoke Greek, although he would never give up Hebrew, his native tongue.

Greek was such an odd and different language. Learning to get the structure correct had been difficult, but over time he'd managed to become quite fluent – although he still had a slight accent. It was because of his fluency in both Hebrew and Greek that he had been selected for the task he was now involved with: translating the holy Hebrew Scriptures into Greek. He and about seventy others had been working on this project for a long time, and it had proven to be a challenging task due to the immense difference between the two languages. Lucius knew that many languages were similar to each other, but such was not the case with Hebrew and Greek.

Hebrew was a lovely metaphorical type language. Nearly all the words were concrete terms, and only a few were abstract. Concrete terms are words used for objects detectable by the human senses. These are things that can be seen, tasted, touched, heard, and smelled; real, tangible objects. Abstract terms, on the other hand, describe ideas, concepts, and emotions; things that have no physical form.

Examples of abstract terms include love, honor, kindness, and other such intangibles. These kinds of terms generally did not exist in the Hebrew language. To Lucius, the absence of abstract terms did not detract from the Hebrew language, but actually served to enrich it. For when one wished to express an abstract concept, one used a concrete term as a metaphor, and in his opinion doing this gave a richer expression to one's communication. His mind went back to the account of when Moses used the concrete term of "heavy" when telling God of his inability to give a good speech. Moses had said, "I am heavy of speech, and heavy of tongue." By using the term "heavy" he had effectively described his lack of eloquence. This was the beauty of Hebrew – it was a rich language full of metaphors.

It seemed to him a pity to take such a rich language and translate it into the comparatively dull and rigid Greek language. But that was his job. As much as it pained him to prepare a work that would inevitably lose the richness of the original text, he knew he must continue the translation. After all, if he didn't do it, there would be somebody else, probably less qualified than himself, who would take up the project. Allowing that to happen would be even more painful than doing the work himself. He simply could not bear the thought of having someone less qualified attempt to bring the holy Hebrew Scriptures into the Greek language.

He picked up his pen. This next phrase was another example of the metaphorical quality of the Hebrew language:

"And he nursed in YHWH, who wove righteousness"

"Righteousness" – one of the few abstract terms in Hebrew. That would be easy to translate. But he found himself scratching his head over the metaphorical terms, trying to decide the best way to translate them. Finally, Lucius set his pen to paper, praying that God was leading him.

> *"And Abram trusted in God, and it was imputed to him for righteousness."*

A few hundred years later, Tertius set down his pen as Paul paused from dictating the letter to the Roman believers. "You know," Paul said, "I thank God for the Septuagint: the translation of the Hebrew Scriptures into the Greek language."

"Me too," agreed Tertius, "I wouldn't even be able to read the Scriptures if they were only available in Hebrew."

"You and untold numbers of Gentile believers," smiled Paul. "Not only that, but it would be ten times more difficult to explain these concepts if I couldn't refer my readers to the inspired Scriptures given to my forefathers! How would I even begin to explain and demonstrate the concept of imputed righteousness? But if they have even a rudimentary knowledge of the holy Greek Scriptures, they will be familiar with these terms and can understand what I am speaking of. Can you imagine how long these letters would be if I had to explain every term in detail?"

"My wrist gets sore just thinking about it," grinned Tertius ruefully, rubbing his wrist as he spoke, getting ready to write some more.

~ ~ ~   ~ ~ ~   ~ ~ ~

More than 1,500 years later, James placed the large volume on the shelf alongside of his other books. There was scarcely enough room to house the volume – he would need another bookcase before too long! This latest book was special. It was the first print edition of what had been years of labor, and was his contribution to English speaking Bible students. "The Exhaustive Concordance" was what he called it, because it was the only one hitherto constructed that gave an index of every word of the King James translation, and of all the passages where they are found.

During its construction, he insisted on keeping in view three great features: completeness, simplicity, and accuracy. His intent was to create a permanent standard for purposes of reference: so full in its vocabulary and lists that everyone consulting it would be sure to find a passage easily and quickly, by seeking it under any word that it contained. At the same time, he wanted it so plain in its arrangement that a child could not miss his way in using it. Finally, his goal was that it would be so correct in its citations, both numerical and verbal, that the most scholarly might implicitly depend upon it.

In pursuit of simplicity, James had recognized that many Bible students were unable to read Greek and Hebrew. To enable the English-speaking students to reference the Greek and Hebrew words, a numbering system was devised: all the original words were arranged in their alphabetical Greek and Hebrew order, and were numbered from the first to the last. Thus, each original word was known throughout the book by its appropriate number. This rendered reference easy without recourse to the Greek characters.

But James Strong had no idea how widely used this numbering system would become. Although the Strong's Exhaustive Concordance he created has been largely replaced by computer searches, the Strong's numbering system lives on. It is not uncommon to see Strong's numbers in biblical reference books.

~ ~ ~   ~ ~ ~   ~ ~ ~

Almost exactly a hundred years after Strong published

his concordance, Charles Van der Pool was hard at work on his monumental contribution to English-speaking Bible students. Before Van der Pool published his work, a Bible student un-versed in the original languages would find it difficult to take one of the significant words used in the Apostle Paul's writings and trace its use in the Septuagint (LXX), the Greek translation of the Old Testament, and thereby gain a richer understanding of its use in a theological context. Previously, the average Bible student was dependent on Greek scholars to explain the significance of Greek terms, but had no method of verifying the fidelity of a scholar's work. What Van der Pool did was link a number to every Greek word in the LXX. He developed the AB-Strong numbering system, which built upon James Strong's numbering system by inserting a decimal in the number for the Greek words found only in the LXX. In addition, he set up his work in an interlinear fashion, giving an English translation in line with the Greek text. This work enables the English student to cross reference Greek words used in the New Testament with their use in the LXX. Words that carry theological significance in the NT can easily be examined in the Old Testament context that Paul and the believers of his day would have been familiar with. In this day of liberal scholarship, the value of this work for the English Bible student cannot be overstated.

~ ~ ~   ~ ~ ~   ~ ~ ~

The intent of this chapter is twofold: to provide the reader with a bit of insight into the Hebrew language, and to give a glimpse of the historical background of the Greek translation of the Hebrew Old Testament.

The Hebrew Language

While there are many obvious differences between the Hebrew language and English, a key difference is the use of abstract and concrete terminology.

The English language contains a large proportion of abstract terms. Abstract terms are words that refer to intangible qualities, ideas, and concepts. These words indicate things we know only through our intellect, like "truth," "honor," "kindness," and "grace." Examples of abstract terms can be found in Psalms 103:8 "The LORD is <u>compassionate</u> and <u>gracious</u>, slow to <u>anger</u>, abounding in <u>love</u>." The underlined words are abstract terms, ideas that cannot be experienced by the senses.

In contrast to English, Hebrew is known as a concrete language, meaning the bulk of its words are concrete terms; it had few abstract terms. Concrete words refer to tangible qualities or characteristics, things that can be seen, touched, smelled, tasted or heard. An example of this can be found in Psalms 1:3; "He is like a <u>tree</u> planted by <u>streams of water</u>, which yields its <u>fruit</u> in season, and whose <u>leaf</u> does not <u>wither</u>."

Those of us who speak only English may wonder how Hebrew-speaking people were able to effectively communicate without using abstract terms. How would one communicate trust (an abstract concept) if one's language did not have a word for trust? The answer is alluded to in the story above: they used their concrete terms as metaphors for abstract concepts.

In his book "The Hebrew Genius as Exhibited in the Old Testament" (2010), George Adam Smith said, "...the Hebrews were mainly a doing and feeling people. Thus, their language has few abstract terms. Rather, Hebrew may be called primarily a language of the senses. The words originally expressed concrete or material things and movements or actions which struck the senses or started the emotions. Only secondarily and in metaphor could they be used to denote abstract or metaphysical ideas." In other words, the Hebrew language made heavy use of metaphors: the concrete terms were commonly used as metaphors for abstract concepts.

An outcome of a having a highly metaphorical language is that the range of meaning for a given word can be very broad, since it can legitimately be used to express both concrete ideas and abstract. However, the metaphorical nature also indicates meanings are related in the same way that a metaphor relates the concrete idea with the abstract. Generally, the metaphor provides vivid imagery to help us understand the abstract idea, as we saw in the story above. Obviously, the context is a key component in identifying the intended meaning of a metaphorical use of a word.

In later chapters, we will find it necessary to perform a word study or two. It is hoped this background of the Hebrew language will aid the reader in understanding the method that will be used.

The Greek Old Testament

It may also be helpful for the reader to be aware of the ancient Greek translation of the Old Testament and understand its relevance for today. This translation was done about 200-300 years before the birth of Christ and is commonly known as the Septuagint, which is Latin for 70. Legend has it that 70 translators were involved in the work of the translation. The common abbreviation for the Septuagint is LXX, the Roman numeral for 70.

The significance of the LXX is that it was widely used among the Jews at the time of Christ, and among the Christians throughout the apostolic era and after. In addition, the New Testament writers readily quoted from it when referencing Old Testament passages. This wide use would have provided a common basis for understanding scriptural concepts, despite inevitable differences between believers with regards to culture, understanding, society, background, and even timeframe. The apostles would have been free to reference concepts or use certain words from the LXX without explanation, knowing that their readers were likely familiar with the LXX.

Therefore, when studying a Greek New Testament word,

the serious Bible student should consider, if possible, the uses of the word in the LXX. This can be especially helpful when there is not enough information given in the context of New Testament passages to help the reader understand the meaning of a significant word. A word study in the LXX was formerly a difficult task for those who, like the author, are not literate in Greek. But now, thanks to Van der Pool's work, English-speaking students have a resource whereby they can identify every place in the LXX where a given word was used and examine each context. The name of this resource is "The Apostolic Bible Polyglot" and it can be found via a search for apostolicBible.com on the Internet. In a truly generous move, Van der Pool has made this valuable resource available for free in PDF format. It can also be purchased online in a hard-copy book format.

Discombobulation

As mentioned before, it will be necessary to perform some word studies in the following chapters. Generally, Strong's numbers will be used throughout this work to refer to the original Greek and Hebrew words instead of inserting the actual Greek and Hebrew words. Although the original words could easily be copied into this work, the author finds that Strong's numbers are easier to keep track of (not to mention easier to pronounce).

Where verses are quoted to give an example of the use of a given Greek or Hebrew word, the verse will be quoted in English and **bold italics** will indicate the location of the word within the verse. Unless otherwise noted, all verse quotations are taken from the New King James Version (NKJV). This is true even for quotations of Old Testament verses that are referenced to illustrate how the LXX used certain words.

When verse quotations are denoted by "LXX," the quotation is taken from the Apostolic Bible Polyglot (ABP). The ABP is an English translation with a Greek interlinear gloss where the numbers and Greek word appear immediately above the English translation. Thus, the English word order follows the Greek words instead of English grammar. To avoid confusion, Van der Pool numbered English words according to the order they would have if they followed English grammar. See the following verse as an example:

> And I shall shake all the nations. And [⁶ shall come ¹ the ² chosen ³ of all ⁴ the ⁵ nations], and I will fill this house [with] glory, says [the] LORD almighty. (Haggai 2:7, LXX)

When verses such as these are quoted within this work, the brackets will be removed and the word order adjusted according to the numbering. See the following example:

> And I shall shake all the nations. And the chosen of all the nations shall come, and I will fill this house with glory, says the LORD almighty. (Haggai 2:7, LXX)

2

Introducing Election

Will the Real Election Please Step Forward?

Greetings. It is a pleasure to meet you. My name is Election. Sometimes I am called Elect, and sometimes Chosen depending on the context and who is speaking. Anyhow, I want to thank you for taking the time to get to know me for who I am. Over the years I have seen many people mistakenly assume they knew me well. Some embraced me as if I were a trophy, or held me aloft like a theological banner. But there are others who cringe when I enter a room as if they preferred I didn't exist. They avert their eyes and refuse to look at me, as if I were an enemy who would capture and imprison them if they looked directly at me. But I'm not a monster. In fact, I think if those who feared me knew me for who I am, they would love me and rejoice to be with me.

Not that I blame people for disliking me. If I were actually like what many people claim, I wouldn't want to share a room with myself either. I've seen what some people have said about me, and to be honest, I don't know where these definitions originated. But there seems to be a growing trend among people to assume these definitions are true and accurate portrayals of who I am. Do you know what definitions I'm talking about? They go something like this, "Elect: chosen, chosen by God: to obtain salvation." I have seen this kind of definition on multiple websites, in many commentaries, and increasingly in study Bibles. Even some dictionaries will slip in a definition like this. But I tell you, that isn't me.

Or at least, it *wasn't* me. I realize that as a member of a living language, my definition may change over time. Once a definition begins to stick to a word, it kind of defines who we are. But, as a member of the Greek language, "chosen by God for salvation" was not a definition I originally carried. That definition was attached to me sometime after the Holy Scriptures were completed. Looking back, I can see it was after I was given that definition that people began to dislike and avoid me. So, I really appreciate you taking the time to look a little closer at me and perhaps begin to see the beauty God intended to display in me.

Where to start in explaining who I really am? I think maybe a good starting point is to share that, as a scriptural Greek word, I had three forms. Scholars tell me that my original form was that of a simple verb, an action word. From my verb form (eklegomai) came an adjective (eklektos), and then a noun (eklogē). Similar to many other words, each of my forms were closely related but carried different connotations. Please don't feel that you need to memorize the Greek words, for I will reference each form using the associated Strong's number. In some ways, numbers are easier to keep track of, and maybe a little easier to understand (especially if you are not familiar with Greek).

Verb Form

My Greek verb form was assigned the number G1586. As a typical verb, I described an action performed by an individual. The action I described was a choice, a selection. Not just any random choice, mind you, but a deliberate and careful selection of an object for one's self. Of course, having limited scope regarding the type of choice I described reduced the number of times I was used in Scripture, but I don't mind. I'm not the type of word that feels the need to be used all over the place. In my opinion, the more frequently a word is used, the less intrigue it has. Besides, I am used more frequently than some of the other words, such as "Propitiation."

As I was saying, my verb form described a deliberate choice. An example of this kind of choice is in the story of Lot when he separated from Abram. After evaluating the surrounding region, Lot **chose** (that's my verb form!) the plains of Jordan for himself. You can see that I didn't bother with the little choices of life. I described the big, significant choices, where careful consideration was involved. Of course, Lot's choice turned out to be a poor one, but I didn't discriminate on the quality of the choice I described, so long as it had significance.

On occasion, I have had the honor of being used to describe a choice made by God Himself. Actually, not to brag, but, more than once I was called upon to describe God's choices. A few examples include the choice of Aaron to be the priest, and the choice of Jerusalem as a place where He would set His name. There was also His choice of the twelve apostles. Oh yes, and the choice of Israel as the people of God. That was a big choice. There were a few other choices, but there was one choice that Scripture never employed me to describe, and that was: the choice of certain individuals to receive righteousness or salvation. I imagine that will surprise some people, but it's true. I will not expand on this now, but it will be discussed in greater detail later on.

Adjective Form

Moving on to my adjective form, it was given the Strong's number of G1588. Typical of adjectives, this form was used to describe an object, to make clear the type of object. If one didn't know better, one might predict that my adjective was used to describe an object as a selected object. For example, the chosen plains of Jordan; that is, the selected plains. Indeed, there were occasions when my adjective form was used in this way, but they were rare. Instead, my adjective usually described an object as desirable, something that would certainly be selected if there was a choice to be made. For example, it wasn't normally used to indicate the selected plains of Jordan, but the choice plains of Jordan that were of high quality and desirable.

When my adjective form was applied to people, it often described them as being valued and favored. An example is when I had the honor of describing the very Son of God, in the passage where God spoke of His **elect** (that is my adjective!) Servant, in whom He delighted (Isaiah 42:1). You can see that I was not merely indicating that the Servant was selected. I was conveying the treasured status of the Servant in the sight of God, for the Servant was favored by God above all others. It seems that despite being frequently used in this way, this element of my adjective is commonly overlooked. Thus, many have assumed that when Scripture used me to describe believers as God's elect, I was saying that they were selected by God. But the reality is that I was referring to the fact that they were treasured and people in whom God delighted. Personally, I think if this aspect of me had greater emphasis, more people would enjoy having my presence in their conversations.

Noun Form

Finally, my noun form is heavily derived from my verb and adjective forms, as you might expect. This form was given the Strong's number of G1589. I was not as widely used in this form as in the other two forms. But, as a noun, I was used exclusively to speak of God's selections of people. Since my verb was a deliberate selection of significance, and my adjective described objects as favored, then it follows that my noun spoke of a deliberate selection of favored objects. And so it did. As a noun, I usually spoke of God's selection of people whom He had chosen for Himself. There were and are two classes of people who enjoyed this kind of selection: the nation of Israel, and the believers in Jesus Christ.

Although much remains to be said, my intent was to give you a brief summary of who I am in the Scriptures. As a verb, I told of a deliberate choice. My adjective form described something that was highly valued. The mixture of these two forms made up my noun form, which referred to a people whom God deliberately chose as His treasure.

I hope you found this a pleasant portrait, even though it is but a rough sketch. The following articles will fill out my portrait in greater detail, using Bible stories to illustrate each of my forms. Each of the stories are followed by word study summaries which uncover my definitions. Sadly, I will be leaving you at this juncture, but hopefully this simple introduction has piqued your interest enough to further explore my identity on your own in the following chapters.

3

CHOSEN BY GOD

Not Arbitrary

"He says on the other side of the front veil is unparalleled beauty!"

"I can imagine," I replied excitedly. "Did he tell you what it looks like?" I had never been behind the front veil, and I was eager to know what it was like. Abishua, my best friend (and second or third cousin) had never been back there either, but his dad was Phineas, the priest, and he got to go behind the veil of the Tabernacle on a regular basis. I was trying to get Abishua to tell me everything he had heard from his dad about what it was like to be in the Tabernacle, behind the front veil.

"Well," answered Abishua, "You know the golden lampstand?" I nodded as he continued, "He says the seven lamps on it are kept burning brightly, and their light makes all the gold on the inside of the Tabernacle sparkle! The polished golden walls make it look like a hundred lamps are in there, while the table and incense altar glimmer and shine like they have a light of their own."

"That must be spectacular," I said, trying to imagine what it would be like to be in a room where everything was covered with gold. "Not only would it be amazing to see but imagine what it would be like to actually be inside the Tabernacle, right next to the living God of Israel! What do you suppose it is like to be on the inside, close to God?" I asked.

Abishua knew what I meant. "Dad says it is the scariest and the most thrilling place to be. He says he can hardly believe that on the other side of the inner veil is the presence of our holy God."

I wanted to know more and was about to ask if his dad ever talked to God while he was in there. But just then Abishua's mother called to him to come home. "Do you think your dad would take me in there for a quick peek?" I asked hopefully, even though I knew the answer.

"No," said Abishua, "You aren't of the family of Aaron."

"I know, I know. Why do you suppose it is like that? Why can't I go into God's Tabernacle and be in His presence?" I asked. I wasn't really grumbling, but wishing with all my heart that I could go in there. "Why can't I buy the best ram ever from the marketplace, and go through the cleansing ritual and become a priest like your dad? I'd love to be able to minister in the presence of God."

Abishua looked thoughtfully at me. "Hmm," he said, "I don't know. I guess I never asked Dad that." Just then, his mom called again, so we had to cut our conversation short, but I didn't stop thinking about it.

Later that night, in the cool of the evening after dinner, I went to Dad as he sat by our front doorway. My dad was a leader of our tribe, and he usually sat there in the evening in case anyone wanted to talk to him about tribal issues. No one was with him that evening, so I pulled up a stool and sat down beside him. After a minute or so, I said, "Dad, can I ask you a question?"

He looked at me, smiling, and said, "Sure. What's on your mind?"

I could see he was in a good mood, so I went ahead and asked, "Dad, is the family of Aaron more special or holy than our family?"

He looked at me thoughtfully for a minute, then answered,

"No, I don't think so, son. They are of the tribe of Levi, just as we are. And even if we were not of the tribe of Levi, the whole nation was made holy before God when we were sprinkled with the blood at the foot of Mt. Sinai. I think if you were to ask one of the priests, they would not say they are more holy than we are."

I rocked on my stool, wondering if I should ask my next question. Then Dad said, "Why do you ask?"

Steadying my stool, I gathered my courage and asked my question: "Why do they get to enter the Tabernacle and our family does not?"

Dad turned and looked at me, his face unreadable. I began to wonder if I shouldn't have asked the question. But after a bit, he said, "That's a good question, Son. I suppose it is that way because Moses commanded it to be so."

As I thought about this, hope began to fill me. Moses was an old man. Maybe the next leader would allow our family to minister inside the tabernacle. So I asked, "Do you think that things will change after Moses dies?"

Dad responded, "Why should it be after he dies?" I didn't understand what he was saying at the time, but I could tell that was all he was going to say, so I didn't ask any more questions. It wasn't until later that I found out what he meant, and I also found out that he was horribly incorrect: things were not the way they were because Moses had commanded it to be so.

It was a couple of weeks after our conversation that my dad became well known among the nation of Israel. What he did, and the events that took place were published in the national media. I've inserted clippings from the articles below because it still is a little difficult for me to talk about what happened.

Wilderness Daily News

Several leading men of the tribes of Israel have called on Moses and Aaron to resign as the Heads of State over Israel. Korah Bar-Izhar, a Levite noble, along with Dathan and Abiram Bar-Eliab, and On Bar-Peleth, nobles from the tribe of Rueben, have called for an administrative change. These men, along with 250 nobles representing the whole of the congregation of Israel, have gone to Moses and Aaron demanding that they submit to the will of the people by resigning from their self-appointed positions and allowing the nation to select new leadership.

Late yesterday morning, Korah and the 250 nobles came to Moses and Aaron to lodge a formal complaint regarding Moses and Aaron's assumed authority over the nation. They contend that Moses and Aaron do not have any inherent right to hold the position of sole representatives for the nation before God. Arguing that God has made the whole nation holy, they asserted that any representative chosen by the nation would be fit to go before God. While acknowledging that the nation had at one time selected Moses and Aaron as official representatives, the nobles accused the two leaders of abusing the nation's trust and elevating themselves above the people. To curb the alleged abuse of the position, Korah and the nobles are now demanding that Moses and Aaron resign. "You take too much upon yourselves," said Korah to Moses, "For all the congregation is holy, every one of them, and the Lord is among them. Why then do you exalt yourselves above the assembly of the Lord?"

Initially, Moses' response to the allegations was one of apparent shock, causing him to fall on his face before Korah and the nobles. However, he was soon able to recover and respond to Korah and the nobles. It appears that Moses will not mount a resistance to the demands of the people. Although he agreed to begin negotiations on the morrow, he insisted that such negotiations should take place before the Tabernacle of Meeting. Korah agreed, and the talks are scheduled to be held later today before the Lord at the Tabernacle.

Moses, however, insisted it was not the people's right to choose their representation. "Tomorrow morning the Lord will show who is His and who is holy, and will cause him to come near to Him," said Moses to Korah. "That one whom He chooses He will cause to come near to Him." One of Moses' staff, who requested his name be withheld, stated that Moses' position is that the LORD reserves the right to select the representation of Israel and only persons chosen by the LORD would be allowed to approach Him.

Korah and the 250 nobles have agreed to meet Moses in front of the Tabernacle later today. Each man will carry a holy censor and present themselves before the LORD to see if there is any preference on the part of the LORD as to who should be the new representative. "It shall be," said Moses, "that the man whom the Lord chooses is the holy one."

When asked who would be fit to approach God as representative of the nation, a spokesman from Korah's office pointed out that at Mt. Sinai, God said He would make the nation a holy people. It is Korah's position that the sanctification has been accomplished through sacrifices and rituals, and thus any member of the nation is fit to approach God. Korah believes that Levites would be best suited for the task since they are trained in how to perform all the rituals of the Tabernacle. However, should he be selected as the nation's representative, he intends to provide the necessary training to any interested Israelite so that any qualified person could have the opportunity to become the representative.

An official response was issued by Moses to Korah only minutes before press time and is published below in its entirety.

"Hear now, you sons of Levi: Is it a small thing to you that the God of Israel has separated you from the congregation of Israel, to bring you near to Himself, to do the work of the tabernacle of the Lord, and to stand before the congregation to serve them; and that He has brought you near to Himself, you and all your brethren, the sons of Levi, with you? And are you seeking the priesthood also? Therefore, you and all your company are gathered together against the Lord. And what is Aaron that you complain against him?"

Moses and Aaron have functioned as the nation's representatives before God since the days when Israel was at the foot of Mt. Sinai. In those days, when the glory of God appeared before the people, the nation recognized that they were unfit to approach God and asked Moses to speak to God on their behalf. Shortly after, Moses appointed Aaron, his brother, as high priest, and the two have acted as the nation's representatives to God ever since. However, in recent times the two men have incurred increasing public disapproval due to unpopular commands they have imposed upon the people. Polls have indicated the recent decision to turn away from the border of the promised land and return to the wilderness was highly unpopular. Up to 75% of those polled indicated a strong displeasure with the direction the nation is headed and were favorable to a change of representation.

Dathan, Abiram, and On were not present at the confrontation but remained at their homes in a statement of disregard to the authority of Moses and Aaron.

EXTRA, EXTRA!

Over 250 nobles of Israel have died in an afternoon of terror.

In accordance with the agreement from the previous day, Korah Bar-Izhar and 250 nobles of the children of Israel met Moses and Aaron in front of the Tabernacle of Meeting to select the new leadership. A large crowd also gathered to witness the historic occasion.

The nobles each prepared holy censors with incense and stood at attention before the Lord. Suddenly, an exceedingly bright light burst from the Tabernacle, evidently being the glory of the Lord. Aaron and Moses turned toward the glory and appeared to be speaking with the glory when they suddenly fell on their faces. Remaining prostrate for a brief minute, they suddenly arose and ran away from the Tabernacle crying out, "Clear yourselves away from their tents!" The elders of Israel followed the two leaders along with some members of the press.

The 250 nobles remained with their censors before the Tabernacle, apparently assuming that Moses and Aaron had conceded the representation and leadership to Korah and the nobles.

However, Moses and Aaron went directly to the tents of Dathan and Abiram and warned the people to evacuate the vicinity of the tents. "Depart now from the tents of these wicked men!" cried Moses to the bystanders, "Touch nothing of theirs, lest you be consumed in all their sins." Not daring to offend Moses, the people backed away, while Dathan and Abiram defiantly remained with their families at their doorways, warning Moses not to start anything. After the people had moved away from the tents, Moses uttered these chilling words:

"By this you shall know that the Lord has sent me to do all these works, for I have not done them of my own will. If these men die naturally like all men, or if they are visited by the common fate of all men, then the Lord has not sent me. But if the Lord creates a new thing, and the earth opens its mouth and swallows them up with all that belongs to them, and they go down alive into the pit, then you will understand that these men have rejected the Lord."

Immediately, massive sinkholes opened beneath the tents of Dathan, Abiram, and Korah. The tents, along with the men, their families, and all their possessions fell into the gaping holes. Pandemonium broke out as people fled from the sinkholes, but the holes collapsed as quickly as they had formed. Rescue crews have been frantically working all afternoon, but at press time there was no success at the recovery of either the men or their possessions.

At the same time as the appearance of the sinkholes, a fire erupted from the Tabernacle and consumed the 250 nobles at the Tabernacle with their censors. All 250 nobles are confirmed dead.

For the time being, Moses and Aaron continue to act as the leaders of Israel.

A PLAGUE OF DEATH killed thousands of protesters and was heroically stopped by Aaron.

Late yesterday morning, a large crowd of protesters, estimated to be in the tens of thousands, came against Moses and Aaron and accused them of bringing death upon the nobles of the people of God. Thousands chanted, "You have killed the people of the Lord." Choosing not to confront the mob, Aaron and Moses turned to go to the Tabernacle of Meeting, but the angry mob followed them, refusing to depart.

At the Tabernacle, the cloud suddenly appeared with the glory of God. Aaron and Moses instantly fell on their faces before God. Suddenly, Aaron jumped up and hurried inside the Tabernacle courtyard. While he was inside, people within the angry crowd began to die, evidently struck by a plague of death from God. The plague proceeded to spread rapidly, and thousands were dying. Some died even as they tried to flee from the expanding area of the plague.

The plague was brought to a stop when Aaron ran out from the courtyard with a burning censor in his hand, having lit it with fire from the altar. Bravely, he ran to where the plague was spreading and positioned himself between the dead and the living. Incredibly, the plague stopped and did not go past him.

At last count, the number of people who died in the plague was 14,700 and included members of the press, one of which was the former editor of this paper. The number would surely have increased if Aaron had not risked his life at the edge of the plague.

GOD HAS MADE KNOWN HIS WILL: Aaron, and thereby the tribe of Levi, have been unquestionably chosen as ministers in the service of God and the representatives of the nation.

After the devastating results of Korah's challenge against Moses and Aaron, the Lord instructed Moses to collect a staff from each of the 12 heads of the tribes of Israel. Each staff was given a clear mark of identification and placed before the Lord in the Tabernacle overnight. The Lord said that blossoms would appear on the rod of the man whom He had chosen to be the representative for the nation. The blossoms and almonds which appeared on Aaron's staff this morning make clear the choice of the Lord: Aaron and his descendants have been chosen by the Lord to be holy and without blame before Him, serving the nation as priests. If any other person attempts to approach the Lord, they will not only be rejected; they will die.

Along with Aaron, the entire tribe of Levi has been chosen from among the nation to perform the service of the Lord, although they will not be coming before the Lord in the same manner as Aaron and his descendants. They will retain this position throughout their generations, for God has chosen them.

My father had completely misunderstood the situation, and it cost him his life. It was not because of Moses' command that the family of Aaron approached God, for it was not Moses who was in charge. It was God who had chosen the family of Aaron to approach before Him. We, as mere men, were foolish to think that we could tell God how it should be. He is the living God of heaven and earth. When we rebelled against Moses and Aaron, we were rebelling against God. It is a wonder that He did not destroy the whole lot of us. Not only has He spared us, but He has also allowed my family to continue to minister before Him at the Tabernacle. True, I will never see the inside of the Tabernacle in all its glory, but it is enough to have the privilege of ministering to the living and holy God right at the door of His holy Tabernacle.

Perhaps you are wondering if I ever try to talk to Him through the Tabernacle walls. The answer is no, I don't. Somehow, it doesn't seem quite appropriate to talk to God as if He were a man. But I do often sing before Him. You might think it odd that I sing, but sometimes I can't contain the wonder of it all. I, who should have been destroyed along with my father Korah, have instead been chosen to minister before Him as one who is holy and without blame. I think if you were in my position, you might find yourself singing His praises too!

~ ~ ~ ~ ~ ~ ~ ~ ~

The sad story of Korah, Dathan, and Abiram is recorded in Numbers 16-18. In reading the account in Scripture, one might get the impression that Korah's family perished along with him, but Numbers 26:11 clarified that Korah's children did not perish with him. As you may have guessed, the above chapter was written from the perspective of a son of Korah with the purpose of illustrating the concept of God's deliberate choice. This concept will be explored in the following chapter.

4

Chose

Deliberate Selection

Blessed be the God and Father of our Lord Jesus Christ,
who has blessed us with every spiritual blessing
in the heavenly places in Christ,
just as He chose us in Him
before the foundation of the world,
that we should be holy and without blame before Him
in love
Ephesians 1:3-4

These opening verses in the letter to the Ephesians begin a paragraph of praise which vividly describes the good blessings God has poured out on us. Although we know these opening verses were intended to be a joyful benediction to our God of blessing, sometimes we may find our joy is tempered because of the central phrase "chose us in Him." This is because we are aware that the Greek word for "chose" is closely related to the Greek word translated "elect," and that relation has often resulted in this passage becoming a theological battleground instead of a field of rejoicing.

Instead of avoiding the point of contention, let us boldly face the main issue and take a close look at the Greek word for "chose." Let us search out the word through all the pages of Scripture to see how it was used and what it meant. Let us honestly seek out its true definition, delineate it, and then apply it to this passage. Let us seek the truth, and not avoid it.

In researching the meaning of a word, a natural place to begin would be to look at the definitions in the lexicons. However, given the scholarly contention over this word, we may question our ability to discern whether the lexicons are giving us an unbiased opinion of the word's meaning. We would undoubtedly feel safer if we could somehow verify the lexicon definitions. Of course, the best method for testing a word definition from a lexicon is to carefully look at how Scripture used the word over a number of contexts. While it is beyond the scope of this book to present a highly detailed study, we will look at a summary of a word study on the Greek word "chose."

The Greek word Paul used in Ephesians 1:4, translated "chose," is a verb. The word also has an adjective form and a noun form. Listed below is each form of the word, along with their associated Strong's numbers and a brief, basic definition.

> **G1586** **eklegomai:** Verb; To choose, select, choose for oneself.
> G1588 eklektos: Adjective, derived from G1586; The chosen, select, elect.
> G1589 eklogē: Noun, derived from G1586; The choice, selection, election.

The definitions of the three words are related, and we will examine each word, attempting to gain a clear understanding of their definitions based on scriptural use while hopefully avoiding theological bias.

G1586: To Choose

The Greek verb represented by the Strong's number, G1586, was not a narrowly defined word. It was used in a broad spectrum of contexts throughout the Greek Old Testament (LXX) and the New Testament (NT). In fact, it apparently was as versatile a word as our English word, "chose." Similar to the English word, G1586 was used to refer to choosing a wide variety of things, such as:

- God choosing the nation of Israel,
- God choosing Saul as king,
- The people choosing Saul as king,
- David choosing five stones for the battle with Goliath,
- Saul choosing soldiers for battle,
- Joshua's call to the people to choose whom they would serve,
- Lot choosing the plains of Jordan,
- The prophets of Baal choosing their bull,
- A man choosing a log to make into an image,
- Etc.

Not only was G1586 as versatile as "chose," but it was also similar in meaning: the act of picking out or selecting from multiple possibilities. However, the lexicons tell us that G1586 indicated a specific type of choice: that of a careful, deliberate selection. It did not indicate an arbitrary or random selection.

To illustrate the type of selection, imagine a man shopping in the marketplace for a melon. Suppose he comes down the aisle to the display of melons and arbitrarily grabs the melon nearest him for purchase. It would not be appropriate to use G1586 in describing this type of selection. However, if the man approached the display and carefully evaluated several of the melons before finally making his choice, then G1586 would be appropriate to use.

As mentioned above, G1586 enjoyed broad use throughout the LXX. It is beyond the scope of this book to examine each and every context in the Scriptures where G1586 occurred. Instead, we will narrow the focus to the contexts involving God's choosing. Even in this reduced scope, the number of passages is significant, but we can group all of God's major choices into the following categories of chosen objects: priests, city, ministers, people, and apostles. It is within the scope of this book to briefly look at each of these categories in turn.

As we look at the categories of God's choosing, we will find there were three or four elements consistently present in each one.

1. We might readily anticipate the first element of God's choosing: there was always a clearly defined set of chosen items or individuals. In contrast to a random choice of arbitrary items, a careful and deliberate choice is normally expected to have clearly defined items or individuals.

2. The second element was a definite purpose or function which the chosen were to fulfill. This element is not surprising since it would be odd to have no purpose in mind for deliberately chosen items or individuals.

3. The third element of God's deliberate choice was a certain permanence of choice. This element comes from the character and person of God. He knew the end from the beginning, saw the public things and the secret, and was intimately acquainted with the innermost parts of a man. When God made a choice, He was fully aware of every implication. He was never surprised by a choice which didn't turn out the way He intended. Therefore, it should be no surprise that when God made a deliberate choice, it was permanent in nature.

4. The fourth element is that the chosen objects became holy unto God. This was true in most contexts of God's choice, although there were one or two exceptions. Often,

when God made a deliberate choice, He was choosing items or individuals for His purpose and use. Thus, these objects were made holy because, by definition, any object set apart for God's use is holy.

Noting these elements within each category of God's choice should help us gain a clear understanding of G1586, and enable us to arrive at a clear interpretation of Ephesians 1:4.

Category A: Chosen Priests

In the LXX, G1586 was used multiple times to refer to the choice of God regarding who would be priests, although it is perhaps the story of Korah that most clearly draws the reader's attention to the deliberate nature of His choice.

> For the LORD your God has **chosen** [Aaron] out of all your tribes to stand to minister in the name of the LORD, him and his sons forever. (Deuteronomy 18:5)

> Did I not **choose** him out of all the tribes of Israel to be My priest, to offer upon My altar, to burn incense, and to wear an ephod before Me? (1 Samuel 2:28a)

In this category, the first element of God's choice (the identification of the chosen), included Aaron and his sons. As we saw in the story of Korah, this was a clearly defined choice of God, and deliberate. It was **clearly defined** in the sense that there was no mistaking God's intention about who was chosen. It was **deliberate** in the sense that no other family could replace the family of Aaron, as Korah so painfully discovered. It was a **choice** in the sense that Aaron's family was selected from among the myriad families in the nation.

The second element, the purpose for which they were chosen, was identified as the role and function of the priesthood. It was not that God chose Aaron's family above everyone else for some greater level of blessing (such as an increased portion of the promised land, or greater riches), but that God intended for Aaron's family to fulfill the specific purpose of functioning as priests.

The third element, regarding the permanence of His choice, was clearly stated in the above verse, "...the LORD your God has chosen... him and his sons forever." In other words, as long as there was a priesthood in Israel, the priests would be of the family of Aaron.

The final element, a position of holiness, can easily be shown as true in this context. The priests were made holy unto the Lord, and He gave considerable instruction on how the holiness was to be established and maintained.

Category B: Chosen City

Several times in Deuteronomy, G1586 was used to speak of a specific place where God would set His name, although it was not until the days of David that the city of Jerusalem was revealed as the identity of the place.

> "Since the day that I brought My people out of the land of Egypt, I have **chosen** no city from any tribe of Israel in which to build a house, that My name might be there, nor did I **choose** any man to be a ruler over My people Israel. Yet I have **chosen** Jerusalem, that My name may be there, and I have **chosen** David to be over My people Israel." (2 Chronicles 6:5-6)

In this category, the clearly defined choice was Jerusalem, selected from among all the cities of Israel. God selected it for the purpose and function of being the place where He would set His name. Although it does not specifically say so in this particular passage, from the rest of Scripture we know that Jerusalem was the chosen city forever – there would be no other city where God would set His name. Finally, Nehemiah referred to Jerusalem as a holy city (see Nehemiah 11:1). Thus, similar to the previous category, all four elements were present in this category of God's choice.

In addition to the choice of a city, there was a second choice referenced in the passage above: David (chosen individual) as king over Israel (purpose). In 2 Samuel 7:16 God speaks of establishing David's throne forever, but we do not find anywhere that he was specifically called holy unto God.

Category C: Chosen Ministers

While the nation of Israel was in the wilderness, God chose a certain group of individuals for the service of the tabernacle. David spoke of this choice in the following passage.

> Then David said, "No one may carry the ark of God but the Levites, for the LORD has **chosen** them to carry the ark of God and to minister before Him forever." (1 Chronicles 15:2)

In this category, the clearly defined choice was the Levites, selected from among all the tribes of Israel. God selected them for the purpose and function of performing the ministry and service of the Lord in the Tabernacle. This choice was also permanent and not subject to change. Finally, the Levites were considered holy unto the Lord. As in the previous categories, so in this one we see all four elements present.

Category D: Chosen People

Moses spent a significant amount of time expounding to the children of Israel their status before God, using G1586 to describe them as God's chosen people.

> For you are a holy people to the LORD your God, and the LORD has **chosen** you to be a people for Himself, a special treasure above all the peoples who are on the face of in the earth. (Deuteronomy 14:2)

> For You have made Your people Israel Your very own people forever; and You, Lord, have become their God. (1 Chronicles 17:22)

God's clearly defined choice was the nation of Israel, selected from all the nations of the earth. The purpose for which God selected them was to be His people, as a special treasure, and His inheritance. The choice was unchanging, as Paul pointed out in Romans 11:1-2. Moreover, they were certainly counted a holy people unto God.

Category E: Chosen Apostles

The New Testament used G1586 in the telling of how Jesus chose twelve disciples as His apostles.

> And when it was day, He called His disciples to Himself; and from them He **chose** twelve whom He also named apostles: (Luke 6:13)

At this point in the Lord's ministry, Luke recorded that the Lord had spent the whole night in prayer. In the morning, He called all His disciples to Himself. We do not know how many disciples He had, only that from this group He selected twelve men. Thus, in this category of God's choice, the clearly defined selection was the twelve men named in Luke 6:14, selected from among all the Lord's disciples. Christ selected them for the purpose of acting as His apostles. Eventually they were commissioned to go out and preach the gospel of the kingdom throughout all of Israel (Luke 9:1-2). The choice was permanent: they all remained apostles until the day they died. However, regarding the fourth element, they are not referred to as holy in the Scripture until Ephesians 3:5.

Interestingly, when the eleven disciples determined a need to fill the office left open by Judas Iscariot, they employed G1586 when they brought the matter before the Lord.

> And they prayed and said, "You, O Lord, who know the hearts of all, show which of these two You have **chosen**... (Acts 1:24)

They did not make the same mistake as Korah and attempt to fill the office with a person of their choosing but looked to the Lord to indicate whom He had chosen.

Ephesians 1

Before returning to Ephesians 1, let us pause and get our bearings by tabulating a summary of our discussion thus far.

Category	Purpose	Duration	Holy
Aaron and sons	To be priests	Forever	Yes
Jerusalem	Place to set His name	Forever	Yes
Levites	Carry the ark	Forever	Yes
Israel	To be God's people	Forever	Yes

Category	Purpose	Duration	Holy
The 12 disciples	To be apostles	Lifelong	Yes

As we consider the categories of God's choosing, we might notice that there were two types of purpose for which God chose people. The first was for a ministry or service. Aaron and his sons were chosen to minister as priests; the Levites ministered in the service of the tabernacle; David served as king; the disciples served as apostles. However, the nation of Israel was chosen, not primarily to serve God but to be His people. God chose them for Himself, as His special treasure on the earth. Thus, we see God chose people either for a particular ministry or for Himself.

For as often as the idea of salvation is linked to this word, it may be surprising to note that none of the surveyed categories of God's choice spoke of individuals chosen to be saved. In fact, each of these categories of chosen included unsaved individuals.

- Category A: Aaron's sons died before the Lord after their inauguration as priests, and Eli's sons died for their ungodliness.

- Category B: The Lord wept over Jerusalem because of their rejection of the Gospel.

- Category C: All the Levites were not godly (recall Korah).

- Category D: The nation of Israel was often inundated with ungodly men.

- Category E: Even among the twelve, Jesus said: "Did I not **choose** you, the twelve, and one of you is a devil?" (John 6:70).

In these categories, God's choosing was not an indication or a determination of the individual's salvation. Nor was God's choosing an indication of suitability or competence for fulfilling the purpose of the choice.

- Category A: As the fabricator of the golden calf, Aaron was completely unqualified to take the role as high priest. However, God made him a priest, fit to approach Him.

- Category B: Jerusalem was not the greatest or most beautiful of cities, but she received the greatest honor when the God of the universe set His name on her.

- Category C: The Levites descended from a man who helped slaughter an entire city. Because of this cruel act, Jacob prophesied that they would be scattered among the other tribes. God made them ministers of His holy things and keepers of His holy dwelling.

- Category D: The nation of Israel was small and insignificant among the nations, but they were elevated above all nations as the chosen people of God.

- Category E: In the gospels, we see the twelve were not exceptional men but came from the same stock as the rest of us. However, they were called to go before the Messiah and announce His approach.

In each category, God did not make His choice based on merit or ability. In the riches of His goodness, He chose ones who were unfit then provided what was needed to make them fit and acceptable for the purpose which He had in mind. The choice of God is truly a demonstration of unmerited grace: there is no one generous like our God.

Given the observations above, we should expect to find in Ephesians 1:3-4 a clearly defined chosen object and an expressly named purpose, along with an element of permanence and perhaps holiness.

> ...just as He **chose** us in Him before the foundation of the world, that we should be holy and without blame before Him in love... (Ephesians 1:4)

Clearly, the chosen object is "us." However, who was "us?" The writers of the epistle? Or did the apostle intend to include the Ephesian believers? Or, was the intent to include every believing reader of these words?

Leaving this question for the moment, let us uncover the purpose for which "us" was chosen. Was it that before the foundation of the world God chose certain ones to be saved? The answer is clearly in the negative, for the verse does not say, "He chose us *to be* in Him (Christ)..." That is, it does not state that the purpose of God's choosing was for certain individuals to be placed in Christ, i.e., to be saved. What is stated as the purpose of God's choice is "...that we should be holy and without blame..." From this, it should be clear that the purpose for which "us" was chosen is for "us" to be holy and without blame. In other words, certain individuals were chosen to be holy and without blame before the holy God.

At first glance, being "holy and without blame" may appear to be synonymous with being saved. However, as mentioned above, there were many categories of people in the Old Testament who were made holy apart from salvation, such as Aaron's sons as priests, the Levites (including Korah), and the nation of Israel. Thus, the purpose of God expressed in Ephesians 1 is that certain individuals will be made holy unto Him in the same sense as those made holy under the covenant of Law – they will be separated out from all other classes of people unto God.

Having identified the purpose for the choice, perhaps it is now more easily seen that the verse does reveal the identity of "us." As noted above, the verse does not read "...He chose us to be in Him..." – it reads that "...He chose us in Him..." Surely it is clear that the chosen is not merely "us," but "us in Him." Of course, we readily understand that "us in Him" are people who have been saved and are in Christ. Thus, the verse is saying God made a selection of the people who are in Christ, for the purpose that they should be holy and without blame. In other words, God has chosen all those who are saved in Christ to be holy and without blame.

Paul was telling the reader that all people who are in Christ, both Jew and Gentile, were chosen to be holy and without blame before God. In Ephesians 2, Paul reminded the Gentiles of former times when they were "aliens from the commonwealth of Israel and strangers from the covenants of promise, having no hope and without God in the world." In those former times, the Israelites were chosen to be the holy people of God, and the Gentiles were considered common and unclean. However, he wrote, now in Christ Jesus:

> ... you are no longer strangers and foreigners, but fellow citizens with the saints and members of the household of God, having been built on the foundation of the apostles and prophets, Jesus Christ Himself being the chief cornerstone, in whom the whole building, being fitted together, grows into a holy temple in the Lord, in whom you also are being built together for a dwelling place of God in the Spirit. (Ephesians 2:19-22)

Notice how Paul took great care to emphasize the point that there was only one body in Christ, made up of both Jews and Gentiles. He reiterated the point in Chapter 3.

> ... by revelation He made known to me the mystery... which in other ages was not made known to the sons of men, as it has now been revealed by the Spirit to His holy apostles and prophets: that the Gentiles should be fellow heirs, of the same body, and partakers of His promise in Christ through the gospel... (Ephesians 3:3-6)

Having pressed home his point of one body of believers, he then brought out the truth that this grand work of God was not an alternative plan B. He wrote that it had once been a hidden plan, but was now revealed as being the master plan from the very beginning.

> To me, who am less than the least of all the saints, this grace was given, that I should preach among the Gentiles the unsearchable riches of Christ, and to make all see what is the fellowship of the mystery, which from the beginning of the ages has been hidden in God who created all things through Jesus Christ; to the intent that now the manifold wisdom of God might be made known by the church to the principalities and powers in the heavenly places, according to the eternal purpose which He accomplished in Christ Jesus our Lord, in whom we have boldness and access with confidence through faith in Him. (Ephesians 3:8-12)

In this way, Paul brought the train of thought full circle – by coming back to the thought of a plan established before the foundation of the world. The progression of thought from Chapter 1 to Chapter 3 is that from the very beginning, even the foundation of the world, God had chosen those in Christ, both Jew and Gentile, to be holy and without blame, so that they might be fellow heirs, of the same body, and partakers of the promise in Christ. Thus, Ephesians 1:4 served not only as an introduction but also as a precursor of the climax expressed in Ephesians 3:8-12: the glorious purpose which God accomplished in Christ.

Thus, consistent with its use in the LXX, G1586 was not used here to speak of individuals chosen for salvation. It spoke of those who had been saved and were in Christ, that they were chosen to be a holy people unto God. The word was used to indicate God's purpose for those who have been saved.

Conclusion

When the Scripture used G1586 to speak of God choosing, it spoke of God making a deliberate and unchanging choice of specific individuals (or things) for which there was a clearly defined purpose. Never was G1586 used to speak of God choosing someone to be saved from the judgment of their sins. In fact, in the survey of the categories of God's choosing, we can see that only one category included no unsaved persons: the group spoken of in Ephesians 1:4 – those who were in Christ.

It is clear that this chapter does not exhaustively demonstrate that G1586 was never used to speak of God's choice of someone to be saved. For this reason, an appendix has been attached which lists each occurrence of the word in both the LXX and the NT. Any who desire to verify the absence of this choice in Scripture may find the appendix helpful.

Coda

There is one additional occurrence of G1586 in the New Testament that needs examination.

> And unless the Lord had shortened those days, no flesh would be saved; but for the elect's sake, whom He **chose**, He shortened the days. (Mark 13:20)

It is clear that the chosen objects are the elect. But who are the elect? The Greek word for "elect" has the Strong's number of G1588, and this word is the topic of the following chapters. It is the author's humble opinion that it is best to leave the study of this occurrence of G1586, and the interpretation of this verse, for a later chapter.

However, before we dive into the study of G1588, the author feels it would be beneficial to explore a bit of background material, as it may help clarify key concepts within the word study. Isaiah 65 and 66 used G1588 in a unique manner that appeared to affect the common understanding of the word. So we shall take a short detour into those chapters before beginning in earnest the study of G1588.

5

THE NEW ELECT

A Remnant Foretold

"I was sought by those who did not ask for Me; I was found by those who did not seek Me.
I said, 'Here I am, here I am,' to a nation that was not called by My name."

We were reading the last section of Isaiah's latest so-called prophecy to the king and I remember that he stopped us at this point to inquire about the identity of the nation mentioned in the last line. The king was an educated man and could have read the prophecy himself, but as his advisors, we wanted to make sure he understood the prophecy in the proper, scholarly light. For this reason, we were reading the prophecy to him, providing our educated interpretation as we read. You see, for some reason unknown to us, there continued to be a debate among the common, uneducated masses regarding the validity of Isaiah as a prophet. To us, it was clear Isaiah was a false and harmful prophet, but it was a continual struggle to ensure the king did not fall under the sway of his ravings.

In response to the king's query, we gave our scholarly opinion that this appeared to be the beginning words of Isaiah's efforts to undermine the patriotic national spirit, and thereby begin to incite rebellion against the throne. "It is our opinion, O king," we said with all due reverence, "that Isaiah is attempting to persuade the people that Judah is no longer a special nation before God and that God is going to raise up a new people. Our concern is that if the general populace began to listen to his words, they potentially could abandon their loyalty to the throne of Israel and begin to seek some new kingdom."

The king gave us a look of incredulous disbelief regarding our interpretation, but we begged him to have patience and listen further.

> *"I have stretched out My hands all day long*
> *to a rebellious people,*
> *Who walk in a way that is not good,*
> *according to their own thoughts;*
> *A people who provoke Me to anger*
> *continually to My face;*
> *Who sacrifice in gardens,*
> *and burn incense on altars of brick;*
> *Who sit among the graves,*
> *and spend the night in the tombs;*
> *Who eat swine's flesh,*
> *and the broth of abominable things is in their vessels;*
> *Who say, 'Keep to yourself, do not come near me,*
> *for I am holier than you!'"*

The king could clearly see this was written against the nation of Judah. He was an intelligent young man who had, for the most part, abandoned the outdated notion of monotheism, and had actively promoted the polytheistic worship of the modern age. For some reason, despite his enlightenment, he continued to have regard for Isaiah. Of course, it was rather insulting to have Isaiah compare us, practitioners of the contemporary worship, with those who eat swine's flesh, but Isaiah was one of those ultra-conservative prophets who continually spoke out against progressive concepts.

Although we were accustomed to his hate speech, it was becoming rather tiresome, and for this reason we attempted to stir the king into action against Isaiah.

> *These are smoke in My nostrils,*
> *a fire that burns all the day.*
> *"Behold, it is written before Me:*
> *I will not keep silence, but will repay—*
> *Even repay into their bosom – your iniquities and the iniquities of your fathers together,"*
> *Says the Lord, "Who have burned incense on the mountains and blasphemed Me on the hills;*
> *Therefore I will measure their former work into their bosom."*

I think the king actually yawned at this point, for he had heard Isaiah's rhetoric of the coming judgment time and time again. "God will pour out His judgment upon you because of your terrible sins," was his oft-repeated message. "I thought you claimed Isaiah was trying to stir up rebellion?" said the king, "This is nothing different from what he has ever said. I assume the next paragraph will be telling us that only a remnant will be saved, according to his usual methods."

"Very nearly," we confirmed, "But this, O king, is where his message begins to diverge from his regular custom. He now begins to write of a remnant which has a separate and distinct identity from the nation of Judah. Please, listen as we continue reading."

> *Thus says the Lord:*
> *"As the new wine is found in the cluster,*
> *and one says, 'Do not destroy it, for a blessing is in it,'*
> *So will I do for My servants' sake,*
> *that I may not destroy them all.*
> *I will bring forth descendants from Jacob,*
> *and from Judah an heir of My mountains;*

My elect shall inherit it,
and My servants shall dwell there.
Sharon shall be a fold of flocks,
and the Valley of Achor a place for herds to lie down,
For My people who have sought Me."

At first, the king didn't see our point, and I suppose at first glance it does appear that Isaiah was speaking of the usual remnant of Israel. "But," we said to the king, "If you carefully examine, you will see that Isaiah does not say, 'I will bring forth Jacob, and Judah will be an heir of My mountains.' He speaks of descendants of Jacob, and an heir out of Judah. In other words, it will not be Jacob and Judah, but a new group that comes out from them. And you see, O king, that he calls this new group 'elect' and 'My servants'? As you know, these are terms which rightly belong to Israel and Judah, and Isaiah is ascribing them to a new group of people."

"Hmm. Perhaps," said the king, doubtful. "But who do you think these people are?"

"Excellent and perceptive question, our liege. Isaiah is careless and does not hide from us the answer. Listen to the last line again, 'For My people who have sought Me.' He claims that God is going to make a significant change. The nations of Israel and Judah will no longer be the elect and the servants of God. It will only be the people who follow Isaiah in his intolerance of the worship of gods from the surrounding nations." The king still looked doubtful, but we requested patience, assuring him that Isaiah's rebellious agenda would become increasingly apparent as we resumed reading. We continued:

"But you are those who forsake the Lord,
who forget My holy mountain,
Who prepare a table for Gad,
and who furnish a drink offering for Meni.
Therefore I will number you for the sword,
and you shall all bow down to the slaughter;
Because, when I called, you did not answer;

when I spoke, you did not hear,
But did evil before My eyes,
and chose that in which I do not delight."

"You see how Isaiah is threatening God's judgment on the enlightened Jews who have embraced the broad worship of all gods?" we asked.

"Of course," replied the king, "but he has always warned of God's judgment on the nation for the so-called idolatry."

"With all due respect, your majesty, we believe this is different," we insisted, "for he does not speak of judgment upon the nation as a whole, but of judgment upon a fragmented kingdom: he calls for God's judgment upon only those who worship the other gods. Please, listen to this next part; we believe his agenda becomes crystal clear."

Therefore thus says the Lord God:
"Behold, My servants shall eat,
but you shall be hungry;
Behold, My servants shall drink,
but you shall be thirsty;
Behold, My servants shall rejoice,
but you shall be ashamed;
Behold, My servants shall sing for joy of heart,
but you shall cry for sorrow of heart,
And wail for grief of spirit.
You shall leave your name as a curse to My chosen;
For the Lord God will slay you,
and call His servants by another name;
So that he who blesses himself in the earth
shall bless himself in the God of truth;
And he who swears in the earth
shall swear by the God of truth;
Because the former's troubles are forgotten,
and because they are hidden from My eyes."

"'My servants shall eat and drink, but you shall be hungry,'" mused the king. "That doesn't sound like a united nation. And did I hear his claim correctly that God will remove the everlasting blessing of Judah, making us a curse?"

"Not that He would make the entire nation a curse, O wise one, but only those who give honor to the other gods. It is a division of the people of God."

"I see," said the king with a darkening brow. "To attempt to divide the kingdom is nigh unto treason against the throne!"

The king was beginning to respond the way we wanted. Isaiah had long been a thorn in our side, continually turning the people against our efforts to diversify and expand religious practices. "O king," we said, feigning sorrow, "His rhetoric worsens."

> *"For behold, I create new heavens and a new earth;*
> *and the former shall not be remembered*
> *or come to mind.*
> *But be glad and rejoice forever in what I create;*
> *"For behold, I create Jerusalem as a rejoicing,*
> *and her people a joy.*
> *I will rejoice in Jerusalem, and joy in My people;*
> *The voice of weeping shall no longer be heard in her,*
> *nor the voice of crying."*

Pausing from our reading, we pointed out to the king, "He asserts that God will abandon or destroy this heaven and earth, and He will create a new heaven and earth, and a new Jerusalem. This is, we believe, blasphemy against the very God he claims to speak for. Has not God said that Jerusalem is His city forever, and Judah will dwell in this land forever? In this Isaiah cannot be speaking the truth, for it would be a contradiction."

The king looked stunned. "Are you saying Isaiah has become a lying, false prophet? Surely he speaks of a refurbished earth!"

"We think not, O king, for he describes a whole new quality of life that is entirely unknown to this earth."

"No more shall an infant from there live but a few
days, nor an old man who has not fulfilled his days;
For the child shall die one hundred years old, but the
sinner being one hundred years old shall be accursed.
They shall build houses and inhabit them;
they shall plant vineyards and eat their fruit.
They shall not build and another inhabit;
they shall not plant and another eat;
For as the days of a tree,
so shall be the days of My people,
And My elect shall long enjoy the work of their hands.
They shall not labor in vain,
nor bring forth children for trouble;
For they shall be the descendants of the blessed of
the Lord, and their offspring with them."

Again pausing our reading, we briefly said, "Notice how he claimed that only these newly elect ones will inhabit this new earth." The king appeared to have no comment, so we continued.

"It shall come to pass that before they call, I will answer;
And while they are still speaking, I will hear.
The wolf and the lamb shall feed together, the lion
shall eat straw like the ox,
And dust shall be the serpent's food.
They shall not hurt nor destroy in all My holy mountain,"
says the Lord.

"That sounds like an appealing new earth," said the king.

"Which is why it is so dangerous," we warned, "It appeals to the people who are not as wise and enlightened as you, and persuades them to follow him. But it gets even worse."

Thus says the Lord: "Heaven is My throne,
and earth is My footstool.
Where is the house that you will build Me?
And where is the place of My rest?
For all those things My hand has made,
and all those things exist," says the Lord.

The king suddenly laughed, saying, "He claims that God will abandon His own temple, which He said He would dwell in forever? What utter nonsense!"

"Your majesty, great and wise, it is worse than nonsense. Isaiah is blaspheming the very temple of God with these words."

"But on this one will I look:
On him who is poor and of a contrite spirit,
and who trembles at My word."

"Amnesty," said the king, "He promises them amnesty if they but turn from idols. Clever."

"He makes the people believe that merely by repenting they can become the new elect," we agreed. "Next, you will see Isaiah blaspheme the temple sacrifices and rituals by saying that God despises those who offer them."

"He who kills a bull is as if he slays a man;
he who sacrifices a lamb, as if he breaks a dog's neck;
He who offers a grain offering, as if he offers swine's
blood; he who burns incense, as if he blesses an idol.
Just as they have chosen their own ways,
and their soul delights in their abominations,
So will I choose their delusions,
and bring their fears on them;
Because, when I called, no one answered,
when I spoke they did not hear;
But they did evil before My eyes,

and chose that in which I do not delight."

Grinding his teeth, the king exclaimed, "Does he never tire of condemning the enlightened ways of worship?"

"Apparently not," we replied, "Now hear how he strengthens his movement by deceiving his followers into believing themselves martyrs if any raise their hand against them."

> *"Hear the word of the Lord,*
> *you who tremble at His word:*
> *"Your brethren who hated you,*
> *who cast you out for My name's sake, said,*
> *'Let the Lord be glorified, that we may see your joy.'*
> *But they shall be ashamed."*

By this time, the king was visibly upset. "Confound the man!" he shouted. "He has covered every angle, thwarting me before I can even begin to quench the rebellion!"

We noticed, with some pleasure, his unconscious adoption of the idea of a popular revolution. Things were going very well indeed, better than we had expected. We read the remainder of what Isaiah had written without significant comment until the last paragraph.

> *"For as the new heavens and the new earth which*
> *I will make shall remain before Me," says the Lord,*
> *"So shall your descendants and your name remain."*

"Utter blasphemy!" interrupted the king, "God will never break His everlasting promise with His chosen people of Israel to choose some other mystical group of people."

We couldn't have said it better ourselves, and inwardly we exalted. However, the feeling of exaltation didn't last long. I can't answer for my companions, but I remember being sobered by Isaiah's last few words.

> *"And it shall come to pass*
> *That from one New Moon to another,*
> *and from one Sabbath to another,*
> *All flesh shall come to worship before Me,"*
> *says the Lord.*
> *"And they shall go forth*
> *and look upon the corpses of the men*
> *Who have transgressed against Me.*
> *For their worm does not die,*
> *and their fire is not quenched.*
> *They shall be an abhorrence to all flesh."*

Although these words gave me pause, they only seemed to infuriate the king. "Guards!" he roared, his face contorted with rage, "Arrest Isaiah!"

As we left the council room, I congratulated my companions on our success in ridding ourselves of Isaiah's opposition, while trying to drown out the sound of the ominous last words of Isaiah which were still ringing in my ears.

> *"For their worm does not die,*
> *and their fire is not quenched.*
> *They shall be an abhorrence to all flesh."*

I remember that those were hard words for me to forget. They came back to me when the king had Isaiah brutally executed for his prophecies of judgment. Each time we killed one of Isaiah's followers, I would hear those words as clearly as the day we first read them. Not until we had filled Jerusalem with the blood of those who hated our idols was I finally free from their ominous sound.

Of course, time has shown what fools we were and how right Isaiah was. The nation was carried out of the land, just as he warned in his early prophecies. As he predicted, God did indeed set the nation of Judah aside, taking for Himself a new people who were considered the elect based on their humility before God, and not on their lineage. The prophecy of a new heaven and new earth has also been fulfilled. And those last words, which have continued to ring in my ears over the last few thousand years, they too have been... well, you know...

Anyhow... thanks for hearing my story...

By the way... you wouldn't happen to have a glass of water, would you?

Even if you dipped the tip of your finger in water, it would cool my tongue... for I am tormented in this flame...

~ ~ ~   ~ ~ ~   ~ ~ ~

This story is written from the perspective of one of those mentioned in the last verse of the book of Isaiah, who "go forth and look upon" the men who are in the place where "the worm does not die, and their fire is not quenched." It imagines the individual is listening to a former royal advisor of Manasseh, the wicked king of Judah who reigned during the last years of Isaiah's life. The imaginary advisor is recounting how they read the contents of Isaiah 65 and 66 to the king, giving their interpretation. Although the advisors twisted Isaiah's words, they correctly interpreted that the prophecy told of a new elect; that is, a new people of God, also called a remnant. The story illustrates the change from an election based on national identity to an election based on the attitude within an individual's heart.

6

Elect of God: LXX

Old Testament

And unless the Lord had shortened those days,
no flesh would be saved;
but for the elect's sake,
whom He chose,
He shortened the days.

Mark 13:20

At the close of the chapter on the word study of G1586, the author callously left us hanging in suspense by raising an unanswered question regarding the identity of the elect in the above passage. We will now return to the question by surveying the Greek adjective, which you may recall was derived from the verb form which was translated "chose" in the above verse. The adjective is the second in our list of words related to the concept of election.

G1586 eklegomai: Verb; A deliberate selection for a distinct purpose.

G1588 eklektos: Adjective, derived from G1586; The chosen, select, elect.

G1589 eklogē: Noun, derived from G1586; The choice, selection.

Every occurrence of "elect" in the New Testament (KJV, NJKV, ESV, NASB) was translated from this adjective, so it is clearly an important word with regards to the doctrine of election. Therefore, it is critical that we accurately grasp the meaning of this word if we are to begin to correctly understand the ways of God towards His people with regards to the doctrine of election.

This chapter will focus on the use of the G1588 in the Greek translation of the Old Testament (the LXX). There are a dauntingly large number of passages available to discuss, for the word appeared about 82 times in the LXX. Exploring the detail of each and every context is beyond the scope of this book and probably beyond our level of endurance. We will look at a summary of how the word was used, knowing that an appendix is provided which lists every occurrence for those who want to dig a little deeper.

G1588: Elect, choice

As with the verb form, G1586, so this word, G1588, was used across a broad spectrum of contexts in the LXX. In the same way that G1586 (verb) was used to speak of the choosing of a wide variety of things, so G1588 (adjective) was used as a descriptor of a wide variety of things. Examples of items described by G1588 include tombs, offerings, livestock, trees, soldiers, along with many other items.

We can divide the occurrences of G1588 within the LXX into three groups, for the adjective has three nuances which have distinct, yet related meanings. As we look at each nuance, we will use an illustration to breathe life into the meaning, then review a sample of Scripture texts containing examples. The appendix mentioned above is also broken down into the same three categories of nuance.

Category A: Inherent Qualities

To illustrate this nuance of the word, let us imagine a young man infatuated with a lovely maiden. If we were to ask him what it is about this young lady which he finds attractive, he would blissfully speak to us at length about the beauty of her countenance, her sparkling eyes, the smile on her lips, her grace and feminine form, her delightful conversation and lovely personality, along with all of her characteristics and qualities that have won his heart. As we listen to his glowing description of her attributes and beauties, we very well might be convinced that she is a choice young lady, one in a thousand.

In the last sentence of the illustration, the word "choice" was used as a summary descriptive of the young maiden to indicate that she is a person with excellent qualities. This use serves to illustrate the first nuance of the adjective, G1588. The LXX frequently used the word as a descriptor of people and objects with inherently excellent qualities. An obvious example of this nuance is the first use of the word, found in the context of Abraham obtaining a plot of land in which to bury his wife, Sarah. When he approached the local inhabitants with his request to purchase a burial place, their response contained the use of G1588.

> "Hear us, my lord: You are a mighty prince among us; bury your dead in the **choicest** of our burial places. None of us will withhold from you his burial place, that you may bury your dead." (Genesis 23:6)

In this NKJV translation of this verse, we see the local inhabitants expressed their desire that this mighty prince would have for his use the best of their sepulchers as a burying place.

Keep in mind, the quotation of the verse above is an English translation of the Hebrew Scriptures. The significance is that the English text above conveys the meaning of the original Hebrew text. From our English translation, it is evident the Hebrew text referred to a burial place having inherent qualities which made it superior to other sepulchers. The Hebrew phrasing is significant to us because when the translators converted the passage from Hebrew to Greek, we find they selected G1588 as an appropriate adjective to convey the meaning of the Hebrew text. Since the English translation used "choicest" to convey the essence of the Hebrew, we can assume the Greek word carried a similar meaning (assuming the Greek translators provided an accurate translation). Thus, even we who are illiterate in Greek can easily see that this nuance of G1588 evidently had a meaning similar to "choicest."

If this was the only passage that used G1588 in this sense, one might persuade us that it was an exception to the norm. However, there are many additional passages where G1588 clearly had the meaning of inherent excellent qualities. In fact, this nuance was the predominate use of G1588 throughout the LXX: of the 79 verses where the word occurs, 64 verses used the word to describe the inherent quality of an object. Thus, with regards to quantity, this sense of the word would normally be considered the primary meaning within the LXX.

To give the reader an idea of the variety of contexts in which this nuance of G1588 occurs, a few additional passages are provided below.

> Suddenly there came up out of the river seven cows, fine looking and **fat** [choice]; and they fed in the meadow... And the ugly and gaunt cows ate up the seven fine looking and **fat** [choice] cows. So Pharaoh awoke. He slept and dreamed a second time; and suddenly seven heads of grain came up on one stalk, **plump** [choice] and good... And the seven thin heads devoured the seven **plump**

[choice] and full heads. So Pharaoh awoke, and indeed, it was a dream. (Genesis 41:2-7)

"Also take for yourself **quality** spices – five hundred shekels of liquid myrrh, half as much sweet-smelling cinnamon (two hundred and fifty shekels), two hundred and fifty shekels of sweet-smelling cane," (Exodus 30:23)

All these were the children of Asher, heads of their fathers' houses, **choice** men, mighty men of valor, chief leaders. And they were recorded by genealogies among the army fit for battle; their number was twenty-six thousand. (1 Chronicles 7:40)

The reader is encouraged to reference the appendix for additional passages of this category, for even a quick perusal through the verses will show how often the LXX used G1588 to describing things and people that were superior in some fashion to other similar objects. It is strong evidence that this was the primary sense of the word.

Interestingly, the objects described in this category were not necessarily objects which had undergone a G1586 type of careful selection process, as might have been expected due to G1588 having been derived from G1586. However, one could say the two words are related in the sense that the adjective described objects that surely would be chosen in a G1586 type of selection.

It appears a good definition of this nuance of the word would be one similar to the definitions of the adjective forms of the English words "choice" and "elect," which are as follows:

Choice: (adj.) of excellent quality: "a choice cut of meat."

Elect: (adj.) select or choice: "an elect circle of artists."

This nuance described objects which had inherently excellent qualities. It may be tempting to apply this meaning to the opening verse, and to read it as, "And unless the Lord had shortened those days, no flesh would be saved; but for the [inherently excellent ones'] sake, whom He chose, He shortened the days." However, to do so before exploring the other nuances would be premature.

Category B: Position of Honor

Let us return to the illustration of the infatuated young man. Suppose some time has passed – there has been a proposal, a ring, a lovely ceremony, and a romantic honeymoon. Now the happy couple is returning to their home, which is nothing less than the royal palace. You see, the young man is none other than the crown prince. And who is the young lady? She is now, of course, the princess. However, before her wedding, she was, well, a mere citizen of the kingdom. Her parents were not royalty, and she had no titles to her name. There was nothing in her lineage or accomplishments that would particularly qualify her to be the royal princess – only the fact that the crown prince chose her to be his wife. Because of his choice, she is now elevated in status above all other women in the kingdom, regardless of whatever titles they might possess. The young lady is now choice in a different sense than before. It is not her inherent qualities of lineage or accomplishments that make her a choice young lady, but her position obtained through the selection of the prince.

The use of G1588 in this sense first occurs in the passage when King David asked the Gibeonites what was required for atonement to bring a severe famine to an end. The Gibeonites, as non-Israelites, had greatly suffered under Saul's policies of ethnic cleansing, which contradicted the treaty of protection established in the days of Joshua (Joshua 9). The Gibeonites replied to David:

"Let seven men of [Saul's] descendants be delivered to us, and we will hang them before the LORD in Gibeah of Saul, whom the LORD **chose**." And the king said, "I will give them." (2 Samuel 21:6)

Evidently, they did not use G1588 in this passage with the same nuance as in Category A, which would be to describe Saul as a man with inherently good characteristics. It is true that when he was first chosen as king, he was perceived to have the desirable features of a superior physique. However, the policies he adopted when he was king demonstrated that he was an ungodly character, unfit to be king over the people of God. We see that, instead of describing a man who was choice due to inherent qualities, the Gibeonites were describing a man whom God chose to be king over Israel. They recognized Saul had not become king because of his inherent qualities, but because God had placed him on the throne.

Unlike the broad use of Category A, this sense of the word was only used in the LXX to describe people and not inanimate objects. Furthermore, it was only used to describe people chosen by God for a position of authority, as demonstrated in the following three verses.

Then You spoke in a vision to Your holy one, and said: "I have given help to one who is mighty; I have exalted one **chosen** from the people. I have found My servant David; with My holy oil I have anointed him." (Psalms 89:19-20)

Therefore He said that He would destroy them, had not Moses His **chosen** one stood before Him in the breach, to turn away His wrath, lest He destroy them. (Psalms 106:23)

> And I shall shake all the nations. And the **chosen**
> of all the nations shall come, and I will fill this
> house with glory, says the LORD almighty.
> (Haggai 2:7, LXX)

God chose each of these men for a position of authority. None attained their position by first convincing the general public of their inherent personal qualities of excellence, and then being voted into office. Nor did they achieve their position by their greatness of power. God chose them for their position and established them in it. As far as the author can tell, these four verses are the extent of the use of G1588 with this nuance in both the LXX and the NT.

In Category A, we noted the described objects had not necessarily gone through a G1586 type of selection process. We can see that Category B is distinct from A in that the objects did go through a G1586 kind of selection process in which God deliberately selected each man. Thus, in this category, we see G1588 described people as having been deliberately chosen by God.

As previously noted, God chose each man for a position of authority. A person in authority is typically treated differently from the average person, in that they are given honor and shown respect. Now, it is worth noting that honor and respect are shown not only to people in authority but also to individuals who have inherent excellent qualities of one form or another. For example, sports stars receive honor and respect for their athletic abilities, movie stars for their acting skills, musicians for their talent, soldiers for their courage, engineers for their superior practical intelligence, and so forth. As the public shows honor and respect to talented people, so also do people to individuals in authority.

Of course, we prefer that those in authority over us also possess highly excellent characteristics, but such is not always the case. However, regardless of the quality of their inherent characteristics, we are expected to treat people in authority with honor and respect as if they did inherently have superior excellent features.

Although this nuance is distinct from Category A, we see it is related in the sense that a man described by the Category B nuance of G1588 would receive the same honor and respect as one described by the Category A nuance. In other words, a man placed in a position of authority (Category B) typically expects to receive the same honor and respect as a person who has superior qualities and characteristics (Category A). G1588 acted as a descriptor in both cases.

With regards to Category B, it appears the definition of the English adjective "chosen" is closest to the definition of this nuance of G1588.

> Chosen: (adj.) having been selected as the best or most appropriate: "music is his chosen vocation."

This nuance was used to describe men whom God selected for positions of authority and honor.

Category C: Chosen to be Choice

Some years have passed since the happy honeymoon mentioned above. The young lady is not as young anymore. A few kids have entered the scene, and she expends a tremendous amount of energy trying to keep up with them. Often, when her husband returns home at the end of the day, she is worn out and sometimes even a little bit grouchy. She tries to give him a smile when he comes through the door, but sometimes she just wants to dump the kids on him and wander through the peaceful palace gardens.

Her husband is a good man and is not discouraged by her change from the vibrant young lady of his youth. Some of his wife's youthful attributes which first attracted him have faded with the passing of time and under the responsibilities of life, but his heart is not drawn away from her by the lovely young ladies in the courts of the palace. She probably would no longer qualify as a contestant in a beauty pageant, but he lovingly treasures her above all other women in the kingdom; as far as he is concerned, she is the choicest of women for she is the woman whom he chose to be his own.

This simple illustration demonstrates a nuance clearly distinct from Category A, in that the wife does not, in a general sense, possess the characteristics that typically attract young men to the young ladies. It is also distinct from Category B, in that her position as wife is not a position of broad authority. However, she is honored and treasured by her husband as though she had richer qualities of excellence than all other women, due to his deliberate choice of her as his wife. One could say she was choice to him because he chose her to be his.

This nuance of G1588 occurs only ten times in the LXX. One time it was applied to David, but the other nine times it was applied to the nation of Israel. Sometimes it referred to the nation as a whole, sometimes to a remnant.

> Seek the Lord and His strength;
> Seek His face evermore!
> Remember His marvelous works
> which He has done,
> His wonders, and the judgments of His mouth,
> O seed of Israel His servant,
> You children of Jacob, His **chosen** ones!
> He is the Lord our God;
> His judgments are in all the earth.
> Remember His covenant forever,
> The word which He commanded,
> for a thousand generations,

The covenant which He made with Abraham,
And His oath to Isaac,
And confirmed it to Jacob for a statute,
To Israel for an everlasting covenant,
Saying, "To you I will give the land of Canaan
As the allotment of your inheritance,"
When you were few in number,
Indeed very few, and strangers in it.
When they went from one nation to another,
And from one kingdom to another people,
He permitted no man to do them wrong;
Yes, He rebuked kings for their sakes,
Saying, "Do not touch My anointed ones,
And do My prophets no harm."
(1 Chronicles 16:11-22, Psalm 105:4-15)

These extensive quotes from these mirror passages of 1 Chronicles and the Psalms illustrate the richness of God's favor expressed towards the nation of Israel. Notice how G1588 was not used to describe a nation of excellent qualities, for they were a nation that had often been rebellious. Nor did it describe a nation chosen for a position of authority over other nations, for they were often weak. Instead, it corresponds to the deliberate G1586 choice of the nation of Israel as the people of God. It described a people who were chosen by God to be His own, and were treated by God as though they possessed the highest qualities of excellence even though they were frequently lacking in excellent qualities.

The other passages where G1588 acted as a descriptor of Israel also carried the same flavor of choice-ness surrounding the chosen people of God.

That I may see the benefit of Your **chosen** ones,
that I may rejoice in the gladness of Your nation,

that I may glory with Your inheritance. (Psalms 106:5)

The beast of the field will honor Me, the jackals and the ostriches, because I give waters in the wilderness and rivers in the desert, to give drink to My people, My **chosen**. (Isaiah 43:20)

For Jacob My servant's sake, and Israel My **elect**, I have even called you by your name; I have named you, though you have not known Me. (Isaiah 45:4)

The Old Testament writers clearly indicated that it was counted a blessing and privilege to be among the group of people whom God chose as His own. They saw that the kindness of God towards Israel came as a direct result of God's selection of the nation as His people.

Of the nine times that G1588 described Israel in the context of God's favor, six times it was speaking of the nation as a whole. The covenant God made with Abraham was that He would be God to both him and his descendants, on the condition that they maintained the rite of circumcision. For an Israelite to be included among God's chosen ones, he needed to be circumcised. If he were not, he would be cut off from his people. Because the Israelites were religiously faithful in performing the rite of circumcision, the entire nation was counted as God's chosen people, God's elect.

Notice how the whole nation was counted as God's elect, regardless of their personal standing before God. While it is true that there were many righteous people in the nation, it is also true that there were many ungodly people also. The nation contained both godly and ungodly Israelites, but as a whole, they were the chosen people of God. Thus, in the case of Israel, we see that being one of God's elect was not synonymous with being made righteous. God did not choose them for salvation, but chose them to be His people. As God's chosen people they were often treated as if they had an abundance of excellent qualities.

For many generations, circumcision was the primary requirement to be counted among the chosen. However, in the prophecy of Isaiah 65, a change was foretold from the elect consisting of the whole nation to the elect consisting of only a particular group of people.

> "I will bring forth descendants from Jacob, and from Judah an heir of My mountains; My **elect** shall inherit it, and My servants shall dwell there. Sharon shall be a fold of flocks, and the Valley of Achor a place for herds to lie down, for My people who have sought Me.
>
> "But you are those who forsake the Lord, who forget My holy mountain, who prepare a table for Gad, and who furnish a drink offering for Meni. Therefore I will number you for the sword, and you shall all bow down to the slaughter; because, when I called, you did not answer; when I spoke, you did not hear, but did evil before My eyes, and chose that in which I do not delight." (Isaiah 65:9-12)

The prophecy revealed that much of the nation had long forsaken the Lord and continually chose the very things He hated. For this reason, they, as a nation, would fall from being God's elect. There would be a new elect comprised of people who sought God. In other words, God would take as His people only those who sought after Him. He would no longer be God to those who forsook Him, even though they were descendants of Abraham and circumcised.

Isaiah's prophecy indicated a significant and profound change. For many generations, God had been the God of a stiff-necked people who were continually rebellious against Him. Isaiah foretold that this time would come to a close and God would be the God of a humble people who were of a contrite (repentant) spirit.

> Thus says the Lord: "Heaven is My throne, and earth is My footstool. Where is the house that you will build Me? And where is the place of My rest? For all those things My hand has made, and all those things exist," says the Lord.
>
> "But on this one will I look: on him who is poor and of a contrite spirit, and who trembles at My word." (Isaiah 66:1-2)

For a person to be one of the elect in the day which Isaiah foretold, he would need to be a spiritual descendant of Abraham. Not merely a physical descendant, but one who had the same faith as Abraham and of a humble and contrite spirit. Simply put, Isaiah spoke of a day when only those who had true hearts before God would be God's elect – these alone would be the people of God.

Notice how Isaiah did not say that God would choose certain people, and as a result, they would become humble and contrite. If that had been the case, then the nation of Israel would not have been a stiff-necked and rebellious people, for God chose them. Instead, Isaiah plainly declared that God would look upon the people, and He would show abundant kindnesses to those who had a humble and contrite heart; they would be His chosen people, His elect.

Although this nuance of G1588 is distinct from Category A nuance, yet we can see a connection between the two. Category A described objects as having excellent qualities, and in Category C we see people selected to be treated as though they had excellent qualities, regardless of whether they had those qualities. In other words, God chose them and in His sight they were choice. Thus, it appears a good definition of this nuance of the word might be as follows:

Elect: The chosen (and choice) people of God.

Category D: Chosen for Salvation

Contrary to how G1588 is often defined, this sense of the word does not exist in the LXX. G1588 never described individuals who were chosen by God to receive righteousness. The reader is invited to verify this in the appendix.

What about the following verse?

> But we are bound to give thanks to God always for you, brethren beloved by the Lord, because God from the beginning chose you for salvation through sanctification by the Spirit and belief in the truth (2 Thessalonians 2:13)

This is a significant verse that needs to be addressed. However, the word translated "chose" in this verse is G0138, a word that is unrelated to G1588. The point of this discussion is to examine the meaning of G1588 and the related words. Thus, the above verse is beyond the scope of our study. It will need to be addressed in a different study.

Conclusion

In these days G1588 is commonly defined as indicating individuals selected to obtain salvation, but it was not used that way in the LXX. Instead, it was typically used to describe objects as having inherent excellent qualities. A few times the word appeared in the context of God's selection of individuals to positions of high authority. On a number of occasions, it described a people whom God chose as His people, who enjoyed abundant favor from God. To summarize, G1588 was primarily used either (a) to describe people and objects which had superior qualities, or (b) to refer to the people whom God chose for Himself.

Suppose we take our conclusion and see how it fits within our opening verse, Mark 13:20. If we apply the (b) definition to the verse, it reads, "And unless the Lord had shortened those days, no flesh would be saved; but for the [people of God's] sake, whom He chose, He shortened the days." This reading certainly fits the flow of the verse, and we may be tempted to embrace it and end the discussion at this point. However, to do so would be premature, for although the writers of the New Testament were likely to use G1588 with the same meaning as it had in the LXX, especially when speaking of the people whom God chose, there is the possibility that they used the word in a new sense. However, if they intended a new sense, it would have been necessary to clarify their intent, or they would risk confusing their readers.

For example, suppose an early believer is studying Mark's gospel, and the occurrence of G1588 in Mark 13:20 caught his eye. Wanting to make sure he understands what the Lord was saying, he pulls a current copy of the Modern Dictionary of Greek Words from his bookshelf and flips to the entry for G1588. As he reads the definitions for the nuances of the word, it is certain that he will not find in that secular dictionary a definition that reads: "Individuals chosen by God for salvation."

Suppose that, as our aspiring scholar considers the definitions he found, it occurs to him that a secular dictionary might not be the best resource to discover the theological significance of the Lord's words. Returning the dictionary to the shelf, he takes out his Exhaustive Concordance to the Greek Old Testament and carefully examines every occurrence of G1588. As we have seen above, he would likely conclude that the word could be describing either people with excellent characteristics, or people given a position of honor, or people whom God chose as His own.

However, suppose in using G1588, the Lord meant to describe people chosen by God for salvation. This early believer would have no way of knowing that this was the intended meaning unless Mark made this definition clear in the context.

The next step in this study, therefore, is to examine the uses of the word in the New Testament to see if G1588 clearly received a definition that is different than what we find in the LXX. Then we shall be in a good position to give an educated guess on the identity of the elect in the passage quoted at the beginning of this chapter.

7

GOD'S CHOSEN PEOPLE

Chosen For His Favor

"His place is pretty impressive. It is evident the Romans pay their centurions well."

"I can imagine," I said, excited for our brother, Cornelius, and not the least bit jealous. "Did he give you a tour of the place?" Apelles had just returned from Caesarea where our brother was stationed with his cohort.

"Yes, he did. It is a large place with spacious rooms, but not overly extravagant. The courtyard is bigger than average, bordered with mature shade trees and sitting benches. The floor of the house is elevated and has an impressive stairway with columns at the entry. You go through a pair of big double doors to get into the house. You can definitely see his wife's touch in the interior furnishings. So, it is a beautiful place, but, well, what caught my attention was the changes in Cornelius."

"Really? How so? Is he getting that proud Roman soldier attitude?"

"No, not that. In fact, he is less like a soldier than before." Distractedly, Apelles offered me a bowl full of grape clusters. "He, ah, he prays a lot, and gives money to the poor."

"Cornelius!? Prays?" I laughed and popped a couple of the

grapes in my mouth, "Since when has he started paying attention to the gods?"

"That is what is extraordinary. He doesn't pray to the Roman gods, he prays to the Jewish God."

I nearly choked on my grapes. After a short spasm of coughing, I sputtered, "The God of the Jews! Cornelius?!"

Apelles sympathetically handed me a napkin, "My reaction was similar, except I spewed my wine clear across the table. In short, yes, he has become a worshiper of the God of the Jews. He relayed to me how a few Jewish merchants explained to him the reason for their image-less temple. Apparently, they assert their God is a living God and is the maker of all things. Thus, He dwells in the heavens, not in an earthly temple."

Of course, I'd heard that the Jew's temple had no image. I could not imagine offering sacrifice to empty air. How did they ever know if their God heard them?

"He then shared with me that he had a long conversation with the merchants and it greatly piqued his interest. Some days after the conversation, they returned and gave him a copy of their religious writings. To my surprise, Cornelius claimed he avidly read through all they gave him. Not only that, but he also began attending their synagogue and listening to their teachings."

"Teachings? Like a school?"

"I suppose so."

"What is there to teach about the gods? It's all a bunch of legends."

"Cornelius did share with me some information regarding their teachings. Apparently, the Jews believe their ancient writings originated from their God and therefore they study these Scriptures to learn of His character and person."

"Seriously? They study to learn what their God is like?" That just seemed weird to me. I couldn't believe Cornelius was into something like that.

"That is what Cornelius informed me. My understanding is the Jews think their God is far above humans in power and wisdom. They claim it takes a lifetime to begin to understand and comprehend His ways. Cornelius himself rather enthusiastically stated that their God is amazing. He said he is astonished at His righteousness and holiness, and mercy towards those who seek Him."

"A righteous God? None of the gods are righteous – they are as immoral as humans, or even worse."

"Evidently not the Jewish God. Cornelius showed me many of the laws they received from their God. There is no arguing about the righteousness and justice of the commands they follow. It is evident their God does not practice or even permit a lack of righteousness."

"That's impressive. I can see why that would appeal to Cornelius." I pondered what Apelles told me, then shrugged. "Yeah, well, if this God they worship is the Creator of all things, then surely we can all seek him in our own way."

"I suppose that is true, but Cornelius seems convinced that you can only encounter Him through the teachings of the Jews."

"Really?!" I said scornfully. "And just what makes the Jews so much better than anyone else?"

Apelles said soberly, "Cornelius showed me in their ancient writings the covenant God made with their patriarch, Abraham, to take his descendants as His people. The covenant was that He would be their God, and they would be His people. And it appears He..."

"Wait a second. What do you mean 'they would be His people?' If He is the creator of all things, then aren't we all His people?"

"No, not according to their Scripture writings. Furthermore, it is fascinating to see how history bears out their claim. God made multiple covenants with them, the like of which have never been offered to any other nation. Additionally, they have the holy law of God which declares His commands. Furthermore, at their temple, they perform the sacred service of God. And, they have the solemn promise of God to be established as the head of all nations in the last age. It is rather astonishing to see the level of Cornelius' certainty that the way to the living God is through the Jews."

We sat in silence for a few minutes while I tried to wrap my mind around this concept. It was hard to believe that Cornelius had become convinced that the Jews were the people of God and held a position of honor in the sight of God above all other nations. Truth be told, it was a bit difficult to accept that the Jews were above the Romans in some fashion. However, I knew that the Romans didn't have any special access to the living God. In fact, as far as I knew, they didn't have any access to God at all. "Well," I said, "this is some unexpected news you bring, Apelles. I suppose if Cornelius thinks the Jews have something, then maybe a guy should look into it and see if there is anything to their claims."

Apelles nodded. "Cornelius sent a couple of their books back with me. I've nearly finished with the first and can lend it to you, if you are interested."

I nodded my assent, and the conversation turned to other things.

It took a while, but eventually Apelles and I were convinced that Cornelius had discovered the truth. Through reading the Jewish Scriptures and visiting the synagogue, we too began to see the reality of the God of Heaven. It was all true – God had chosen the nation of Israel as His people and had given them the revelation of Himself. They were the children, and we were the outsiders, mere dogs. Even so, we eagerly ate the crumbs that fell from the children's table and found them far more fulfilling than the emptiness of the idolatry around us.

Then came the day when Apelles returned from a trip from Caesarea full of excitement. While he was there, Cornelius had received a visit from an angel who instructed him to send for Simon Peter. When Peter arrived, Apelles was there with Cornelius to hear what Peter had to say. As Peter relayed the gospel of Jesus, Cornelius and Apelles believed and the Holy Spirit fell upon them and the others with them. As you know, Luke, the physician, recorded the events that took place in his account to Theophilus, so I do not need to repeat them here in detail. Of course, when Apelles told me of the Savior, Jesus of Nazareth, I too believed and received the Holy Spirit.

Immediately thereafter, we noticed significant changes in our lives. The first was the stunning new wealth of meaning we found in the Jewish Scriptures. It was like the heavens had opened and flooded us with a storehouse of "crumbs," although it seemed to us more like a treasure house of jewels than crumbs from a table.

Another change was how we viewed other people. Some of those whom we once had liked, but who didn't embrace our good news of Jesus, became more distant to us. Others, whom we hadn't particularly appreciated, but did welcome the gospel of the Lord, became dear to us. Even with these and other changes, we didn't realize at the time the magnitude of the change that had taken place. Then we received a visit from Peter.

I vividly remember one part of Peter's visit in particular. It was the first day of the week, and we were gathered with the other believers. Peter was quoting from a passage in Isaiah:

"Behold, I lay in Zion a chief cornerstone, elect, precious, and he who believes on Him will by no means be put to shame."

"Them is mighty powerful comfort words," commented Nereus, to whom Greek was a second language. "Jesus, whom precious for God, is very sure person to trust me in."

"True," I replied, "Since God has declared Jesus is the premier and precious cornerstone, then we, who have trusted in Him, need never fear the embarrassment of having misplaced our trust. If God approves of Him, then He is approved."

Nereus nodded as Peter replied, "For this reason, you, who believe that God approves of Him, count Him precious. But to those who do not believe, 'The stone which the builders rejected has become the chief cornerstone,' and He is to them 'A stone of stumbling and a rock of offense.'"

Peter paused, evidently seeing the question on Hermes' face. Hermes, a new believer, hesitantly asked, "You said 'those who do not believe;' are you speaking of the Jews?" As Peter nodded, he continued, "What does it mean that they stumbled? Were they standing at one time and then fell down?"

Apelles moved as if he was about to answer. All eyes turned toward him, and he reddened slightly and glanced at Peter. Seeing Peter smile encouragingly, he turned towards Hermes, saying, "At one time, the Jews did stand before God. When God brought them out of Egypt, He established the nation as a people for Himself. They were His priests to the world, and received God's precepts and statutes. He sanctified them to be a holy nation before Him, separated from the uncleanness of the Gentiles. They were His special people." As Peter nodded his agreement, Apelles continued, "When they rejected the Lord Jesus, they took a position against God. Being opposed to God, it is evident they could no longer be priests unto God. Additionally, having rejected the Holy One, they are no longer holy before God. Thus, they have stumbled from their former position as the special people of God."

Still nodding, Peter added, "They stumble, being disobedient to the word, to which they also were appointed."

"Wait," interjected Hermas, Hermes' brother, "The Jews were appointed to stumble?!"

Apelles looked towards Peter, but he inclined his head toward Apelles and gestured for him to answer. "Yes, many of them were appointed thus because of their rejection. You see, although they were God's special people, many of them obeyed the words of men above the words of God. Our Lord Himself pointed out this discrepancy in their lives, and for this they hated Him. Because of their disobedience to the word of God, they were under the wrath of God. Being under God's condemnation, they could not continue to be the people of God. Eventually, as long as they continued to disobey, they had to fall. Does that make sense?"

As Hermas nodded, Hermes thoughtfully said, "So God made Jesus the breaking point for them."

"Yes," replied Apelles, "Their rejection of Jesus was the point over which God removed them from being His special people. Their priesthood is now empty; it no longer bridges the gap between men and God. They are no longer a holy nation before God."

Even without looking for Peter's confirmation, we could see what Apelles said was true. It was a sobering thought, and we sat in silence pondering their significant loss. Then Peter's face lit up, and he held his arms open towards us, saying, "But now you, who have believed in Jesus, are God's chosen generation. You are a royal priesthood before God. You are a holy nation unto God. You are His special people."

Dumbfounded, we sat stunned, with our mouths hanging open, as the meaning of his words sank in. Then a chorus of questions erupted from the group.

"Us?"

"We are?!"

"You mean..."

"Say what?!"

"My understanding not you!" exclaimed Nereus in his broken Greek.

Smiling broadly, Peter beckoned for silence. As our clamor of voices dropped off, Hermes asked one last question, "Why would God make us, us! His special people?!"

Beaming at him, Peter replied, "So that you may proclaim the praises of Him who called you out of darkness into His marvelous light!"

Softly, in perfect Greek, Nereus said for us all, "Praise be to God!"

Facing all of us, Peter declared, "It is music in my ears to hear God's praises from you, who once were not a people but now are the people of God, who had not obtained mercy but now have obtained mercy."

"How could we help but praise Him," marveled Apelles, "We have been made the elect people of God, chosen for His favor!"

The wonder of it all has not yet left us. We are no longer the little dogs licking up crumbs under the children's table. We have been made the children, seated at God's table, eating the richness of the bread of life! At one time we were without Christ, being aliens from the commonwealth of Israel and strangers from the covenants of promise, having no hope and without God in the world. Now we are no longer strangers and foreigners, but fellow citizens with the saints and members of the household of God. According to His eternal purpose, He has chosen us – we who believe in Jesus – as His special people. In Christ, He has poured out His matchless favor on us.

We are His chosen people! Praise be to our God and Father who has blessed us with every spiritual blessing in the heavenly places in Christ!

~ ~ ~   ~ ~ ~   ~ ~ ~

Let the reader be aware that the above conversation is an attempt to provide a commentary on 1 Peter 2:6-10 without making it look like a commentary. The astute reader will have recognized that, within the conversation, everything Peter said was a near quote of the passage. The things said by the others serve as a commentary to bring out significant points that I believe were intended by Peter when he wrote the passage. As a note of clarification, Peter was not teaching that the church took Israel's place, but that they were made elect in much the same fashion as the nation of Israel was formerly elect.

8

ELECT OF GOD: NT

New Testament

We now take up what is perhaps the most challenging task in our study on the concept of election. Namely, to objectively examine, without bias, the occurrences of G1588 in the New Testament. The primary difficulty seems to originate from our tendency to assume that God's choice of people is inseparably connected with their salvation. We know that all saved people in the New Testament were G1588 (that is, elect). It seems we then infer that all elect people were saved, as if God's choosing did not occur without salvation. For some reason, this connection is hard for many of us to set aside, and that can make it difficult to study the topic objectively.

However, the LXX used G1588 to describe Israel, a nation which we know included a mixture of righteous and ungodly. Obviously, with regards to the nation, being G1588 did not automatically result in salvation. This shows that, within the LXX, being G1588'd and being saved were two distinct states for individuals. While it is true that these states could overlap, they often did not. Thus, we should be willing to allow the possibility that election is a position which is not synonymous with the state of justification.

Given the controversy related to this topic, we will need

to exercise all due diligence to set aside our personal ideas, at least temporarily, and endeavor to objectively examine the occurrences of G1588 in the New Testament. We should be aware that harboring a determination to retain our beliefs without examining all of Scripture may cost us the ability to clearly see the truth.

When Context Doesn't Help

In our survey of G1588 in the LXX, we identified two primary definitions of the word: (1) people or objects which had superior qualities; (2) the chosen (and choice) people of God. We were able to derive these definitions from the narrative passages in the Old Testament, for they provided context which gave a clear indication of what the word meant. However, in this New Testament survey, we will find that the context does not provide the same level of clarity. To illustrate, let us look again at the Lord's use of G1588 in Mark 13:20 and the surrounding context.

For the purpose of the illustration, we will attempt to create a sense of ambiguity regarding the word "elect" by replacing it with "G1588" in the passage.

> And unless the Lord had shortened those days, no flesh would be saved; but for the G1588's sake, whom He chose, He shortened the days. (Mark 13:20)

Suppose we had no idea what G1588 meant and turned to our concise dictionary for some help. Under the heading for G1588, we found multiple possibilities of meaning: (a) elite people, (b) people of God, (c) those selected for salvation, (d) fat cows, or (e) golden chariots. To determine which definition is applicable for this passage, we would need to insert each definition into the verse to see which definitions fit the flow of thought and which disrupt it. So, we copy the verse once for each definition and review each version carefully.

> (a) And unless the Lord had shortened those days, no flesh would be saved; but for the [elite people's] sake, whom He chose, He shortened the days.

> (b) And unless the Lord had shortened those days, no flesh would be saved; but for the [people of God's] sake, whom He chose, He shortened the days.

> (c) And unless the Lord had shortened those days, no flesh would be saved; but for the [selected for salvation people's] sake, whom He chose, He shortened the days.

> (d) And unless the Lord had shortened those days, no flesh would be saved; but for the [fat cows'] sake, whom He chose, He shortened the days.

> (e) And unless the Lord had shortened those days, no flesh would be saved; but for the [golden chariot's] sake, whom He chose, He shortened the days.

We would probably quickly conclude that (e) appears to disrupt the flow of thought, for golden chariots do not consist of flesh. However, regarding (a) through (d), we might conclude that we need additional context, for none of the remaining nuances disrupt the thought flow sufficiently to rule them out.

Suppose we added context, and mentally inserted each nuance as before.

"For in those days there will be tribulation, such as has not been since the beginning of the creation which God created until this time, nor ever shall be. And unless the Lord had shortened those days, no flesh would be saved; but for the G1588's sake, whom He chose, He shortened the days.

"Then if anyone says to you, 'Look, here is the Christ!' or, 'Look, He is there!' do not believe it. For false christs and false prophets will rise and show signs and wonders to deceive, if possible, even the G1588. But take heed; see, I have told you all things beforehand.'"

With this level of context, we could readily rule out "fat cows," since false prophets usually don't spend significant effort trying to deceive the bovine species.

Making a closer examination of the context, we see it stated that God chose the elect, but we do not see the purpose for which He chose them – was it for salvation, or favor, or glory, or something else? Nor do we see the reason why He chose them – was it their inherent qualities, or God's grace, or their faith, or something else? Thus, we are not able to conclusively determine from the immediate context whether (a), (b), or (c) was the intended meaning.

Our exercise showed that the context does not always enable us to derive a definition of G1588. In the above case, we could not conclusively demonstrate a meaning even though we started with a list of possible definitions.

Normal Word Use

In everyday conversation, when someone uses a word that has multiple meanings, typically we understand the word in its ordinary sense. We would not assume a special sense of the word unless there was a clear indication in the context. For example, if you heard your neighbor say he spent the weekend building his cabinet, you could potentially understand his statement two ways. You could assume that he was making a small cupboard with shelves and drawers, or you could think he was assembling a body of advisers. However, you would probably recognize the second definition is a specialized sense that applies to a president selecting advisors. Unless you knew your neighbor was the president-elect, you would likely assume he meant a cupboard, which is the ordinary sense of the word. In the same way, our interpretation of the New Testament should assume terms were used in their normal sense unless the context dictates otherwise.

How are we to know what the normal sense of G1588 was? This question would normally be difficult for us to answer since we live some 2000 years after the writing of the New Testament. However, when we remember that the early Christians considered the LXX as their Scriptures, we can conclude that they would be familiar with how the LXX used the terms therein. Therefore, it is highly likely in the New Testament writings that the normal sense of G1588 would have come from the LXX Scriptures. Thus, in a New Testament context that is ambiguous regarding the meaning of the word, it is reasonable for us to assume one of the definitions from the LXX. Surely if the apostles intended a different meaning, they would have provided clarification in the context.

It is not unreasonable to assume the apostles would clarify their intent when they used a word in a special sense, for we see Paul did this very thing in Romans 3 and 4 with regards to the word "justified." In normal use, "justified" meant: to show or prove a party to be right or reasonable. Psalms 51:4 in the LXX contains an example of the normal use (using the same Greek word as is in Romans).

> Against You, You only, have I sinned, and done this evil in Your sight—that You may be found just [justified] when You speak, and blameless when You judge.

The psalmist was happy to confess his sin so that God would be shown right and reasonable in His judgments. This use agrees with the normal meaning of "justified" throughout the LXX and in multiple places in the New Testament. However, when Paul spoke of "Him who justifies the ungodly" (Rom. 4:5), he did not mean that the ungodly were shown to be right and reasonable in their sin. Surely not! Of course, we are not confused about Paul's intended meaning because, in the context of the passage, he went to great lengths to clarify his intent. Indeed, he was so successful in his clarification that some people today seem to have forgotten the original meaning of the word and, as a result, struggle in interpreting passages where the normal meaning applies.

Method of Approach

As we survey the occurrences of G1588 in the New Testament, we will be looking for the same kind of contextual indication that a new meaning, different from what we saw in the LXX, was applied to the word. In particular, we're interested to see whether any context explicitly gives us the definition of "chosen for salvation" (definition 3). If there is no such indication, then we will evaluate the fit within the context of the two primary definitions of G1588 from the LXX: people and objects which had superior qualities (definition 1); the chosen (and choice) people of God (definition 2). The flow of thought within the context will be used to determine which definition best fits.

Again, our guiding assumption is: if the context is ambiguous regarding the definition of G1588 and there is no indication of a new meaning, then it is likely that the intended meaning was one of the normal nuances found in the LXX.

A quick search in a concordance will reveal that the New Testament used G1588 twenty-three times and, unlike the LXX, it never used the word as a descriptor of inanimate objects. Four times it used G1588 to describe personages other than people, such as the Lord Jesus and the angels, but the remaining 19 times it was used as a descriptor of people. Since it is not possible for the Lord or the angels to be chosen for salvation, then it is these remaining 19 occurrences which will be the focus of our survey.

Gospel Parables

The first two occurrences of the word in the New Testament are in the latter half of the Gospel of Matthew and were each placed in the closing statement of a parable.

> "So the last will be first, and the first last. For many are called, but few **chosen**." (Matthew 20:16)

> "For many are called, but few are **chosen**." (Matthew 22:14)

Matthew 20:16 is in the context of the parable of men hired to work in a vineyard. Some men worked all day, some worked part of a day, but the owner paid all the same wage. Please note that some manuscripts did not include the last sentence of Verse 16. However, regardless of the originality of the phrase, the message of the parable remains the same: it spoke of workers receiving the same pay for different levels of work. We find G1588 at the end of the parable, placed in the context of a call for service, not salvation. Due (in part) to the uncertainty of the authenticity of the phrase, we will refrain from making any conclusions regarding G1588 and move on to the next occurrence.

The second verse, Matthew 22:14, is at the end of the parable of a king who sent invitations to a wedding feast three times. The response to the first invitation was an unwillingness to come by those invited. A second call went out, indicating the oxen had been killed and all things were ready. The responses ranged from disinterest to antagonism: some continued about their business and others killed the messengers. The king was enraged and sent his armies to destroy their city. Finally, a third invitation went out, this time to the highways and byways. The king's servants went out and gathered together all whom they found. Of the many who came to the feast, one individual came without proper wedding attire, and they cast him into outer darkness. "Many are called but few are chosen" is the final sentence of the parable.

The parable was spoken to the Jews in a Jewish context and must be interpreted from the same perspective. Historically, the first invitation to the Jews came while they were in the land of Egypt. They were invited to come feast in the land flowing with milk and honey, but when they reached the border, they turned away in unbelief back to the wilderness. God did not entirely give up on them but worked on preparing the feast for the next several generations. Through Joshua, He removed their enemies and established them in the land. Through David and Solomon, He established His name in Jerusalem and built His temple.

At last, the feast was ready, but ten tribes of Israel had separated themselves from the Temple. So, for many generations, God sent out His servants, the prophets, with an invitation to come, but those invited treated them poorly and killed some. In judgment, God brought the Babylonian armies, destroyed the city of Jerusalem, and scattered the people throughout the world. Still God did not entirely turn His back on the Jews, but once again began sending out His servants with an invitation to His feast. Over many generations, the servants faithfully labored to gather all those they found back to the land of Israel and the rebuilt temple in Jerusalem.

Now God's Son, the King, had come to see the guests who were present for the feast. But not all were ready, for some wore their work clothing instead of wedding garments of joy. Woe to those who were not properly attired, for they would be cast out into darkness. It is at this point the Lord states that many were called, but few are G1588.

The message of the parable was clear, if not startling, to the Jews. Time and time again the invitation had gone out to the nation of Israel. Many, many were called. However, contrary to the popular belief of that day, the nation as a whole would not be received into the kingdom of God. Only a remnant would be received, made up of those who had repented and responded to the call of Jesus. The repentant people, who wore the garments of the joy of forgiveness, were embraced by God as His people; the rest, who wore the garments of works, were cast out.

The only other parable with an occurrence of G1588 is the parable of the widow and the unjust judge. In this parable, the Lord was teaching that His followers should not give up on praying, even though the answer from heaven seemed slow in coming. He spoke of how the widow obtained justice from the unjust judge through her persistence. The Lord closed the parable with the following statement.

> "And shall God not avenge His own **elect** who cry out day and night to Him, though He bears long with them? I tell you that He will avenge them speedily. Nevertheless, when the Son of Man comes, will He really find faith on the earth?" (Luke 18:7-8)

Thus, in this parable, G1588 occurs in a context of the patience of the people of God, for whom God will bring justice. The closing question implies that the elect are those who, in the face of continued silence, still believe in God.

In these three parables, we see that although G1588 was a significant word, it was used almost in passing, without elaboration, and without clear indication (or any indication) of a new meaning. Our next step, then, is to insert the normal definitions from the LXX into the passages and see if either is a likely fit. As noted before, the two definitions are as follows: (1) people and objects which had superior qualities; (2) the chosen (and choice) people of God.

The occurrence of G1588 at the end of the parable of the dissatisfied laborers is difficult to interpret regardless of which definition is used. However, the occurrence at the end of the second parable is clearer. We readily see that the Lord was not saying "many are called but only a few have superior qualities," for those who responded to the invitation came from the highways and byways and obviously were not the elite of society. It makes more sense to understand that out of all the Israelites invited to the feast, only a few were the true people of God, whose hearts were humble and contrite before God.

Equally clear is the statement in the third parable that one day God would avenge not the elite people, but His own special people.

Thus, in these two parables, we see no clear indication of a new definition for G1588. In attempting to apply the two definitions from the LXX, we can probably agree that (2) was more likely the intended meaning than (1) for both parables. Furthermore, we can presumably agree that the definition is a good fit within the context.

If we were to further ponder the Lord's use of G1588 in these parables, we might notice that the Lord used G1588 to distinguish between the true people of God and those who only appeared to be the people of God. Many Jewish people had the outward appearance of being godly, but their hearts were far from God. The Lord distinguished between these outwardly righteous people and those who were pure in heart before God by referring to the latter people as "the elect."

Paul's Epistles

Moving from the parables, we turn to the writings of Paul. Remembering that it was he who went to great lengths to explain what he meant by the term "justify," we have confidence that he would not neglect to do the same with regards to G1588 if it were necessary. The first time he used G1588 was in the crescendo of his discussion which he began in Romans 5.

> What then shall we say to these things? If God is for us, who can be against us? He who did not spare His own Son, but delivered Him up for us all, how shall He not with Him also freely give us all things? Who shall bring a charge against God's **elect**? It is God who justifies. Who is he who condemns? It is Christ who died, and furthermore is also risen, who is even at the right hand of God, who also makes intercession for us. (Romans 8:31-34)

Paul opened the paragraph with his focus on "us," not on the "elect." He used "elect" as a title for "us," but the purpose of his paragraph was not to define or expound on the meaning of G1588. Instead, he used G1588 without any explanation of what it meant as if he assumed his readers were familiar with the word. His passing use of the word implies that a traditional definition was intended.

If we insert the same definition from the LXX that we applied in the parables, we find it does not distort the flow of thought: "Who shall bring a charge against God's [chosen (and choice) people]?" In fact, we find the definition is a perfect fit, for the expression of God's kindnesses and grace towards His people fill the entire passage. Thus, there is no reason for us to use a special definition here.

Paul's only other use of G1588 in Romans is in his greeting to Rufus (*"**elect** in the Lord"* Romans 16:13), which is in a passage of personalized greetings having no clarifying context. So, we will pass on to the next occurrence, found in the letter to the Colossians.

> Do not lie to one another, since you have put off the old man with his deeds, and have put on the new man who is renewed in knowledge according to the image of Him who created him, where there is neither Greek nor Jew, circumcised nor uncircumcised, barbarian, Scythian, slave nor free, but Christ is all and in all.
>
> Therefore, as the **elect** of God, holy and beloved, put on tender mercies, kindness, humility, meekness, longsuffering; bearing with one another, and forgiving one another, if anyone has a complaint against another; even as Christ forgave you, so you also must do. (Colossians 3:9-13)

In this passage, Paul was calling the believers to holy living, and in the surrounding context, he gave much instruction on how the believers were to treat one another. We probably can agree that he did not use G1588 in the sense of definition (1). We probably can also agree that both definitions (2) and (3) could be inserted without disrupting the flow of thought. However, when we look at the context, we do not find Paul expounded on G1588 to explain that he was using the term outside its normal definition. Therefore, it is reasonable to assume he used the word in its normal sense. Our understanding of the passage certainly must be that he was instructing the chosen (and choice) people of God to live in a godly manner, for he gave no reason to think he meant something else.

Moving on to the next occurrence in the New Testament, we find an interesting use of G1588 in Paul's second letter to Timothy.

> Remember that Jesus Christ, of the seed of David, was raised from the dead according to my gospel, for which I suffer trouble as an evil-doer, even to the point of chains; but the word of God is not chained. Therefore I endure all things for the sake of the **elect**, that they also may obtain the salvation which is in Christ Jesus with eternal glory. (2 Timothy 2:8-10)

The more one ponders the above passage, the more interesting it becomes. At first glance, it may appear that "elect" must take on the meaning of "chosen for salvation" in this passage: "Therefore I endure all things for the sake of [those chosen for salvation], that they also may obtain the salvation which is in Christ Jesus." However, upon further reflection, we see this is an impossible rendering, especially when we consider the reason Paul endured suffering – that the elect might obtain salvation. Paul's wording implies that if he did not endure the suffering, some who were G1588 would not obtain salvation. Clearly, "chosen for salvation" is an impossible rendering, for nothing can prevent God from saving someone if He chose them to be saved. Therefore, in this passage, it is highly unlikely that "elect" could mean "people chosen by God for salvation."

Up to this point in our New Testament survey, "elect" has always referred to the people of God. Even within the LXX, we found it was used to refer to God's people. However, at first glance, it appears Paul could not have been using the word in this sense, for why would the people of God need to obtain salvation?

As we consider the context further, we notice Paul attributed the cause of his suffering to two main elements of the message he preached: that Jesus was a descendant of David, and that He rose from the dead. The persecution for this message would have undoubtedly come from the Jews, who were especially offended by these doctrines. Perhaps if Paul had not emphasized these doctrines, he would have avoided much trouble, but he made them the central focus of his preaching in the synagogues. His purpose was not to rile up the Jews, but to deliver the Gospel to those who would hear, that they might be delivered from the bondage of the Law and obtain the salvation in Christ.

With this in mind, perhaps we begin to see how it is that the people of God would need to obtain salvation in Jesus. If we understand Paul as using the term "elect" to refer to godly Jews (and proselytes) who received the Gospel with a humble and contrite heart, then the passage begins to make sense. There were godly Jews in the synagogues at the time Paul went about preaching, who were the true people of God and part of the elect. Because they were godly in heart, if they had died before hearing the Gospel, they would not have gone to eternal perdition, just as their godly fathers, who died before the time of Jesus, did not go to perdition. However, although they were godly, they had not received the salvation which is in Christ Jesus because they had not yet heard the gospel of Jesus. Paul was convinced that despite their godliness, this salvation in Jesus was needful for them, so he endured all things for their sake, that these elect might obtain the salvation in Christ Jesus.

Perhaps it does make sense after all for Paul to speak of the true people of God obtaining salvation in Jesus. It appears he used the term "elect" to distinguish between those who were inwardly godly and those who had a mere outward show of godliness. Reflecting on our earlier discussions, we may realize that not only does it make sense, but it also corresponds with how the LXX used the word and how Jesus used it in the gospels. It appears Paul used G1588 here in the normal sense of the word.

We find Paul's final use of G1588 at the beginning of his epistle to Titus.

> Paul, a bondservant of God and an apostle of Jesus Christ, according to the faith of God's **elect** and the acknowledgment of the truth which accords with godliness, in hope of eternal life which God, who cannot lie, promised before time began, but has in due time manifested His word through preaching, which was committed to me according to the commandment of God our Savior; (Titus 1:1-3)

Paul opened his letter to Titus with a statement that his ministry as a bondservant and apostle was in full agreement with the doctrine of belief held by the elect, and the truth which corresponds with godliness. In other words, his ministry did not contradict their doctrine or godliness. Later in the chapter, he addressed sins in the lives of the believers, such as the lying of the Cretans. He told Titus to rebuke them sharply, for these things were not in accordance with the faith or godliness.

Although Paul referenced God's promise from before the beginning of time, we see he did not take the opportunity to expound on the concept of "elect," nor do we see evidence that he used the word in a special sense. He simply referred to the elect as those who have faith. Furthermore, if we insert the normal sense of "chosen (and choice) people," we find it fits in the context, for it is clear he was referring to the true people of

God. Thus, we again find it reasonable to assume the normal sense of G1588.

In our look at the use of G1588 in Paul's epistles, we have not seen any indication of a new meaning applied. In particular, we do not see any context where "chosen for salvation" was applied to the word. In fact, we uncovered one passage where "chosen for salvation" is a highly improbable, if not impossible, definition of the word. It appears Paul consistently used the word in its normal sense, as would have been commonly understood from the LXX.

Peter's Epistle

If Paul did not give a new meaning to G1588, then perhaps there is some hint of a new definition in Peter's writings. We find Peter used the word in two passages of his first epistle.

> Peter, an apostle of Jesus Christ, to the pilgrims of the Dispersion in Pontus, Galatia, Cappadocia, Asia, and Bithynia, **elect** according to the foreknowledge of God the Father, in sanctification of the Spirit, for obedience and sprinkling of the blood of Jesus Christ: Grace to you and peace be multiplied. (1 Peter 1:1-2)

The structure of this verse in the English translation disguises the fact that "elect" is an adjective. In the Greek, G1588 directly precedes "pilgrims" and reads, "to the elect pilgrims of the Dispersion." In using the word, Peter was describing the type of pilgrims they were: not just any old pilgrims, but elect pilgrims. The reason the translators moved elect out of its place was to communicate the connection between the elect-ness of the pilgrims and the foreknowledge, sanctification, and obedience spoken of in Verse 2. To effectively convey what

Peter said in the Greek, perhaps the verse could be translated as follows.

> Peter, an apostle of Jesus Christ, to the elect pilgrims of the Dispersion in Pontus, Galatia, Cappadocia, Asia, and Bithynia, elect-ones according to the foreknowledge of God the Father, in sanctification of the Spirit, for obedience and sprinkling of the blood of Jesus Christ: Grace to you and peace be multiplied. (1 Peter 1:1-2)

In this passage, Peter alluded to three dynamics of ancient Israel's relationship with God and applied the same dynamics to the pilgrims of the Dispersion. These dynamics were: (a) foreknowledge of God, (b) sanctification, and (c) obedience and sprinkling. Let us pause to consider the significance of these dynamics.

When the children of Israel arrived at Mount Sinai in Exodus 19, God revealed His intent to make them a special treasure to Himself. This special-ness, or elect-ness, was not an emotional spur of the moment but was in full accordance with God's foreknowledge of the nation. In Deuteronomy 32, God revealed His knowledge of their future failures and rebellion. It was with that knowledge in view that He deliberately made them His special people. By his allusion to God's foreknowledge, Peter reminded these elect pilgrims of God's same insight regarding their future when He made them His elect.

The pilgrims' sanctification of the Spirit paralleled the making of the nation of Israel into a consecrated and holy people. However, whereas God sanctified the children of Israel unto Himself through the covenant of the Law, He sanctified these pilgrims through the indwelling of His Holy Spirit.

Finally, the children of Israel were made the people of God for obedience. It was God's intent that they would become a testimony of the rich quality of life under the rule of God through their obedience.

Then, in the same way that God sealed the elect-ness of Israel through the sprinkling of blood (Exodus 24), so the elect pilgrims to whom Peter wrote were sprinkled with Jesus' blood. The reminder of God's faithfulness to the children of Israel must have been a great comfort to the believers, knowing that the position they held was based on greater things than what Israel had!

Later in his epistle, Peter again alluded to the position given to ancient Israel and reminded the pilgrims of the similar, but greater, position given to them.

> But you are a **chosen** race, a royal priesthood, a holy nation, a people for His own possession, that you may proclaim the excellencies of Him who called you out of darkness into His marvelous light; (1 Peter 2:9, ESV)

Here Peter mentioned four descriptive phrases: (a) chosen race, (b) royal priesthood, (c) holy nation, and (d) a people for His own possession. These descriptions came from two passages in the LXX.

> And you shall be to me a (b) royal priesthood, and (c) a holy nation. These words you shall say to the sons of Israel. (Exodus 19:6, LXX, spoken at Mt Sinai)

> The wild beasts of the field shall bless me, sirens and daughters of ostriches; for I established water in the wilderness, and rivers in the waterless place, to give to drink to my (a) chosen

race, (d) my people whom I procured; the ones
to describe my virtues. (Isaiah 43:20-21, LXX)

With these allusions to passages in the LXX, Peter made
a clear parallel between Israel and the Church. Israel was
established as a priesthood and holy nation to make known
the virtues of God. Israel's role before God was a historical
prototype of the Church. Both groups were counted elect for the
same purpose: to provide a witness and testimony to the world
of the glorious excellencies of God. This witness was (and still
is) a crucial testimony because the prevailing lie through the
ages has been that God is not a good God. Since God is not willing
that any should perish, He has chosen a strategy to combat the
lie. This strategy has been to establish certain people in this
world as His people to demonstrate the abundance of His mercy
and goodness so that others might be persuaded to come to
Him. Israel had performed that role in the past, and the Church
performs the function in the present.

As we consider Peter's writing and his allusions to Israel,
it is clear to see he used G1588 to write of the special place the
elect pilgrims had in the sight of God, and how it was similar
to the position held by the nation of Israel. Knowing that in the
LXX, G1588 was applied to Israel to indicate that they were the
chosen (and choice) people of God, it is reasonable to assume
that Peter used the word in the same sense regarding the
believers. It seems doubtful, in a context filled with allusions to
the nation of Israel in the Old Testament, that Peter used G1588
with a different connotation than what we find in the LXX. If he
had, he would undoubtedly have clarified his intended meaning.
However, this he did not do. Therefore, it appears that Peter, like
Paul, used G1588 in its normal sense.

Other Occurrences

The last passage where we find G1588 in the Scriptures is near the end of Revelation.

> "These will make war with the Lamb, and the Lamb will overcome them, for He is Lord of lords and King of kings; and those who are with Him are called, **chosen**, and faithful." (Revelation 17:14)

This verse contains the last occurrence of G1588 in the Holy Scriptures. As with previous passages, so in this verse, the context is ambiguous with regards to the meaning of the word. Surely this implies the author used it in the normal sense. There is certainly no elaboration to indicate a different meaning of the word than what is in the LXX.

The other uses of the word with regards to people found in the New Testament are listed below.

> Greet Rufus, **chosen** in the Lord, and his mother and mine. (Romans 16:13)

> The Elder, To the **elect** lady and her children, whom I love in truth, and not only I, but also all those who have known the truth. (2 John 1:1)

> The children of your **elect** sister greet you. Amen. (2 John 1:13)

There is no need to spend much time on these verses for they simply reference the individuals as elect with no clarification of the word in the context. It is evident there is nothing in these contexts that indicated a special sense of the word.

Matthew and Mark

Our survey of the New Testament use of G1588 is nearly complete, missing only the passages in Matthew and Mark which contain the Lord's prophetic statements regarding His return. Both Gospels record the Lord as having used G1588 three times in His prophecy regarding end times. We will look at both passages simultaneously, as they are nearly identical to each other.

Keep in mind that Matthew's Gospel set the prophecy only two chapters after the parable of the wedding feast. The proximity of these passages would typically lead us to assume that the definition of G1588 in the parable would have carried through to the prophecy, especially since there was no clear indication otherwise. From the earlier discussion of the parable, we recall that the Lord used the term to speak of those who responded to the invitation and came in the proper attire, referring to them as the true people of God.

As you read the following verses, I invite you to take note of how the Lord used G1588 to see if He provided any clarifying remarks on the meaning of the word, or whether He used it in passing.

> "For then there will be great tribulation, such as has not been since the beginning of the world until this time, no, nor ever shall be. And unless those days were shortened, no flesh would be saved; but for the **elect's** sake those days will be shortened.
> "Then if anyone says to you, 'Look, here is the Christ!' or 'There!' do not believe it. For false christs and false prophets will rise and show great signs and wonders to deceive, if possible, even the **elect**. See, I have told you beforehand. (Matthew 24:21-25)

"Immediately after the tribulation of those days the sun will be darkened, and the moon will not give its light; the stars will fall from heaven, and the powers of the heavens will be shaken. Then the sign of the Son of Man will appear in heaven, and then all the tribes of the earth will mourn, and they will see the Son of Man coming on the clouds of heaven with power and great glory. And He will send His angels with a great sound of a trumpet, and they will gather together His **elect** from the four winds, from one end of heaven to the other." (Matthew 24:29-31)

"For in those days there will be tribulation, such as has not been since the beginning of the creation which God created until this time, nor ever shall be. And unless the Lord had shortened those days, no flesh would be saved; but for the **elect's** sake, whom He chose, He shortened the days.

"Then if anyone says to you, 'Look, here is the Christ!' or, 'Look, He is there!' do not believe it. For false christs and false prophets will rise and show signs and wonders to deceive, if possible, even the **elect**. But take heed; see, I have told you all things beforehand.

"But in those days, after that tribulation, the sun will be darkened, and the moon will not give its light; the stars of heaven will fall, and the powers in the heavens will be shaken. Then they will see the Son of Man coming in the clouds with great power and glory. And then He will send His angels, and gather together His **elect** from the four winds, from the farthest part of earth to the farthest part of heaven. (Mark 13:19-27)

Surely it is clear that the Lord used G1588 in these passages without explaining whether He meant "people chosen for salvation" or "chosen (and choice) people." What should our conclusion be? Should we assume that He used "elect" in the sense of people chosen for salvation, contrary to how the rest of Scripture used the term?

Conclusion

We began our survey of G1588 in the New Testament with the goal of finding out if the term had a definition different than those in the LXX: (a) people or objects which had superior qualities; (b) chosen (and choice) people. We noted how Paul applied a special definition to the word "justified" in Romans 3 and 4 and recognized the possibility of a special definition for G1588. However, our survey did not uncover any context that expounded on the term in the same fashion as Paul did with "justified." Nor did we find that any context clashed with the (b) definition from the LXX or indicated the need for a different definition. Surely these findings indicate to us that the New Testament authors used the term in the same sense as did the LXX translators: to indicate those whom God chose for Himself, and their treasured position before Him.

This conclusion raises the question regarding the origin of the definition "chosen for salvation." Although we may not be able to answer the question, it appears the definition was extra-biblical in origin.

Epilogue: Choice vs Pre-selected

At this point, there may be some who are inclined to ask if there is any significant difference between "chosen (and choice) people" and "people pre-selected for salvation." It may seem that for God to choose an individual as one of His people implies that He must also have chosen the person for salvation. The following illustration is offered as an attempt to address this question. It begins as a single example but offers three different endings, each illustrating a different type of selection.

Suppose you were browsing through the shops at the marketplace and the wares of an artistic potter catch your eye. Wandering into the store, you begin chatting with the man behind the counter and discover that he is the creator of all the pottery in the shop. When you inquisitively begin to ask him about his craft, he welcomes you to tour the shop where he does all his work.

As he completes the tour, you happen to notice a shelf in a prominent place displaying a number of beautifully finished pottery pieces. In response to your inquiry, the potter confides that these are vessels he has decided to keep for himself. Intrigued, you carefully examine each piece. To your surprise, you see that they are not more impressive than those on display in the front of the store. "Sir," you tactfully ask, "These are not more colorful than the others you have for sale. Nor are they larger, or more exquisitely formed. Why did you choose to keep these for yourself?"

With a smile, he tells you, "To be honest, it's not easy for me to give up any of the vessels that I make. But when I first opened my shop, I decided that I would only allow myself to keep some of my pottery."

Ending I

Gesturing towards the shelf, he continues, "If you have worked much with clay, you will know that not all clay is the same. Some clay is very responsive and is enjoyable to work with, while other clay requires more work. I've allowed myself to keep the vessels that were good to work with.

"I chose to keep these lovely pieces because of how they responded to my hand while on the wheel. They did not collapse under my applied pressure, nor did they resist being conformed into the shape I desired. They responded beautifully to the pressure I applied and were a joy to work with, so I kept them for myself."

Ending II

Gesturing towards the shelf, he continues, "I obtain my clay from many different sources. These vessels came from clay at the bend in the river where my beloved wife accepted my proposal for marriage. Every year, I make a vessel out of clay from that area and keep it for myself."

Ending III

Gesturing towards the shelf, he continues, "Before I begin working with a particular piece of clay, I set it on the wheel and examine it closely. At some point in the examination, I make a decision to keep or sell the vessel that I will make from it. After I make the decision, I begin to work on the clay to make it into whatever I desire. When I'm done, I sell the pottery that I did not decide to keep, and place on this shelf the ones I decided to keep for myself."

The first ending illustrates the type of God's choosing that we see in the New Testament. God has determined before the foundation of the world that those in Christ will be His people. As we each have experienced, He begins working in our lives long before we believed. As we have seen in other's lives, He also works in the lives of people who never believe. The New Testament indicates that only those who respond to His gentle pressure and believe are made His people.

The second ending corresponds with God's choosing of people that we see in the Old Testament. As illustrated by the potter keeping for himself the vessels that he made of clay from a particular source, so God chose for Himself the people who descended from a particular man, Abraham.

The third ending corresponds with the definition of "chosen for salvation." Based on his knowledge of the clay, the potter made a choice to keep the vessel before he began work. This ending is intended to illustrate the idea that God selected certain individuals while passing over others.

Surely the reader will recognize that there is a difference between the first and the third types of choices. Is it a significant difference? I suppose each reader must judge for himself, but it is the author's opinion that the two types of selection are incompatible.

9

ELECTION: GOD'S SELECTION

The Choice That God Made

The third and final word in our short list of related Greek New Testament words is the noun form of "elect." This word was usually translated "election" in the New Testament.

G1586   eklegomai: Verb; A deliberate selection for a distinct purpose.

G1588   eklektos: Adjective, derived from G1586; The chosen, select, elect.

G1589   **eklogē:** Noun, derived from G1586; The choice, the selection.

Unlike the other two words, G1589 did not occur in the LXX: it was strictly a New Testament word. Nor did it enjoy as broad a use, for there are only seven occurrences in four different passages: Acts 9, Romans 9-11, 1 Thessalonians 1, and 2 Peter 1. With such limited use, we probably do not have enough material to develop a solid definition. However, since it is a noun derived from the verb (G1586), we can be sure it referred to a choice, and we can anticipate that it did not indicate a random choice but a significant, deliberate choice.

Our survey will show that G1589 only referred to a choice

made by God of certain people. It's good to remind ourselves that when G1586 (verb) was used in the LXX to speak of God's choice of people, it spoke of a deliberate choice which had three main features: a clearly defined group of people, an element of permanence, and a definite purpose for the chosen. We recall that the LXX recorded two types of purpose in God's choice of people: to minister before Him, as in the case of the priests, the Levites, and the disciples; and to be His peculiar people, as in the case of the nation of Israel.

As we review the uses of G1589, we will endeavor to apply what we found in the G1586 survey to each occurrence. We will want to see if G1589 referred to a type of choice which corresponded to the type of G1586 choices. If we find one that did not, then we need to determine what kind of choice it referenced.

Acts 9

The Lord called Ananias to go to Saul of Tarsus and told him that Saul was praying and had seen a vision of a man restoring his sight. Knowing who Saul was, Ananias expressed doubt in the man's sincerity and questioned the wisdom of restoring his sight. The Lord used G1589 as He responded to Ananias' concern.

> But the Lord said to him, "Go, for he is a **chosen** vessel of Mine to bear My name before Gentiles, kings, and the children of Israel. For I will show him how many things he must suffer for My name's sake." (Acts 9:15-16)

We see that the Lord told Ananias that Saul was a chosen vessel to bear His name to the Gentiles. The Lord used G1588 to convey that He had not been duped by an empty display of pious and fervent prayers, but had deliberately and knowingly selected Saul as a vessel of witness. Therefore, Ananias had nothing to fear and could rest in the knowledge that the Lord was acutely aware of all aspects of the situation.

In this passage, it is evident that the Lord's choice of Saul was of a similar type to another G1586 choice: His selection of the 12 disciples to be apostles. The twelve were deliberately selected, as was Saul. They were chosen to serve as apostles, as was Saul. They remained as apostles to the day of their death, as did Saul. Thus, we see that this is not a new type of choice, but the same as we have encountered in our earlier study: a selection of an individual to minister in a particular role.

Romans 9-11

At the beginning of this passage, Paul began discussing the reason for the rejection of the gospel by the nation of Israel, who were the people of God. His first point was to show that not all Abraham's descendants were the children of God (Romans 9:6-9). This sad reality was true not only of Abraham's immediate descendants, Isaac and Ishmael, but also of all his descendants. Although they were all called the people of God, they were not all children of God; that is, some of the people of God were very ungodly. After making his first point, Paul then directed the reader's attention to God's deliberate selection of Isaac's younger son over his older son.

> And not only this, but when Rebecca also had conceived by one man, even by our father Isaac (for the children not yet being born, nor having done any good or evil, that the purpose of God according to **election** might stand, not of works but of Him who calls), it was said to her, "The older shall serve the younger." As it is written, "Jacob I have loved, but Esau I have hated." (Romans 9:10-13)

Paul's second point made clear that God deliberately made a selection based on the order of the boys' birth, and not on their character, works, or faith. Thus, the descendants of the younger son were selected to be the people of God in a selection of grace, not a selection of merit. Paul went on in Romans 9 to write of how God's choice resulted in mercy shown to the descendants of the younger son even though they were often ungodly.

These two points begin to answer the question of Israel's rejection of the gospel. The first point revealed that Israel's status as the people of God did not imply that they were all the children of God. Nor did their position indicate that they were all godly, for the second point shows their selection as the people of God was made independent of their lifestyle. Thus, although they all were the people of God, they were not all children of God, and they were not all godly. Therefore, they rejected the One whom God sent in accordance with their ungodliness.

Paul then spent all of Romans 10 placing the blame of Israel's rejection squarely on the shoulders of Israel herself. Israel attempted to establish her righteousness by the works of the Law and rejected the righteousness by faith. The gospel, wrote Paul, was not too difficult for Israel to understand, for the word was near them. Nor were they ineligible for salvation, for the same Lord saves all. Gospel preachers were sent to them, but they did not obey. They heard the message but did not believe. They knew the message was true, for their prophets foretold it. However, in vain did God stretch out His hands to this people, for they were disobedient and contrary. Israel was entirely responsible for her rejection of the gospel.

Closing his discussion of Israel's responsibility, in Romans 11, Paul turned to demonstrate that despite their rejection, God had not wholly discarded the nation of Israel.

God has not cast away His people whom He foreknew. Or do you not know what the Scripture says of Elijah, how he pleads with God against Israel, saying, "Lord, they have killed Your prophets and torn down Your altars, and I alone am left, and they seek my life?" But what does the divine response say to him? "I have reserved for Myself seven thousand men who have not bowed the knee to Baal." Even so then, at this present time there is a remnant according to the **election** of grace. And if by grace, then it is no longer of works; otherwise grace is no longer grace. But if it is of works, it is no longer grace; otherwise work is no longer work. What then? Israel has not obtained what it seeks; but the **elect** have obtained it, and the rest were blinded. (Romans 11:2-7)

Paul referenced the days of Elijah as a historical example of how God had selected a remnant for Himself from among the people of God. At that time, God had assured Elijah that the whole nation would not be lost. A remnant, made up of those who had not bowed to idols, would be saved. Paul wrote that in the same way, God had again selected a remnant of Israelites for Himself from among the nation, this time made up of those who believed the gospel of His Son.

In speaking of the remnant's election of grace, Paul drew a parallel with his earlier reference to Jacob's election of grace. As it had been with their father Jacob, whose election was not based on his works, so it was with the remnant – they were not selected based on their ability to obtain righteousness through the works of the Law. It was an election of grace, not of works. Those who received the righteousness by faith, having confessed Jesus as Lord and believed that He had risen from the dead, were part of the remnant. The rest of the nation, having rejected the righteousness by faith, were made blind.

Regarding their blindness, we should not understand Paul to say that the nation's blindness prevented them from believing the gospel, for their blindness came after their rejection of the Christ. Instead, we should remember the beginning of Romans 9, where Paul wrote of the immense privilege enjoyed by the nation of Israel from the time of Moses until Christ. They had the promises, the covenants, and the law of God. They were conduits through whom flowed the truth of God to the world. However, when they rejected the Son of God, this privilege came to an end. The Israelites, who at one time were God's witnesses to the world, were blinded, to the point where they could not even discern the evident working of God in miracles performed by the apostles (see Acts 5:39).

Having written of God's response to Israel's rejection of the Lord, Paul turned to the topic of Israel's future. He asserted that their rejection of the Lord had not nullified God's original selection of the nation of Israel as the people of God, and revealed that their fall was temporary. In speaking of the nation's fallen state, Paul pointed out that the nation was still the chosen people of God, though they were not part of the believing people of God.

> Concerning the gospel they are enemies for your sake, but concerning the **election** they are beloved for the sake of the fathers. For the gifts and the calling of God are irrevocable. (Romans 11:28-29)

"...they are enemies..." Clearly Paul was referring to the Jews who did not believe, who were antagonistic to the gospel and enemies of those who had obeyed the gospel. However, because they were descendants of Jacob, they were still the chosen nation of God.

God's faithfulness towards Israel should not surprise us, for God is not a man that He would reverse His choice. He chose the nation of Israel fully knowing what the future held. Their rejection of the Son was not a surprise to Him, nor did it alter His intent for the descendants of Abraham. His purpose, clearly stated to Abraham, was to bring blessing to the whole world through them.

As Paul closed his discussion on the future of God's chosen people, the demonstration of the wisdom of God moved him greatly. You may recall that at Mount Sinai, God gave Israel many ritual commands that were designed to teach them the difference between clean and unclean, and through them He revealed the loathsome uncleanness and disobedience of the Gentiles. The Law also exposed their own uncleanness, but it also provided a way to mercy through the cleansing of an atoning substitutionary sacrifice.

Centuries later, God's Son came and called the nation to believe in Himself, but they rejected and disobeyed His words. His crucifixion was used to provide mercy and salvation for the disobedient Gentiles, for God made His death a propitiatory, substitutionary sacrifice. However, the Jews' act of crucifying Him also had the effect of reducing them to the ranks of the disobedient, regardless of their level of ritual cleanness, for they rejected the One sent by God. However, in becoming disobedient, they became eligible for the same mercy shown to the disobedient Gentiles, for the sacrifice of God's Son was expressly for the disobedient. This contemplation in the last paragraph of Romans 11 caused Paul to burst out in praise at the wonders of the riches of the wisdom and knowledge of God in providing salvation for both the people of God and the Gentiles.

In Romans 9-11, Paul used G1589 to speak of two separate selections: the nation of Israel as a whole, and a remnant out of Israel. The choice of the nation of Israel as the people of God was spoken of more than once in the LXX and was not a new concept. Nor was the choice of the remnant, as Paul pointed out in his reference to the days of Elijah. We can see both selections were of the same type – God choosing a people for Himself. The difference between the two was that one group consisted exclusively of children of God who had been made righteous by faith.

1 Thessalonians 1

When Paul heard of the persecution of the Thessalonians, he became concerned regarding their faith. More than once, he attempted to go to them and see how they were doing, but Satan continually hindered him. Finally, he sent Timothy to encourage and establish them in their faith. After receiving Timothy's report of their faith and love, Paul wrote a letter to them expressing his joy and used G1589 in the opening lines.

> We give thanks to God always for you all, making mention of you in our prayers, remembering without ceasing your work of faith, labor of love, and patience of hope in our Lord Jesus Christ in the sight of our God and Father, knowing, beloved brethren, your election by God. For our gospel did not come to you in word only, but also in power, and in the Holy Spirit and in much assurance, as you know what kind of men we were among you for your sake. (1 Thessalonians 1:2-5)

The news of the Thessalonians' persecution had raised a question in Paul's heart regarding these beloved brethren: had they endured, or had their faith been empty? Paul knew eloquent preaching could persuade people to make a decision for Jesus, but the decision would be of no lasting value if God did not receive them. For this reason, Paul had deliberately avoided using eloquence, lest by it he would persuade the Thessalonians to make empty professions. Even so, he was concerned regarding their faith. When Timothy brought back the report of their work of faith, labor of love, and patience of hope, he rejoiced in the clear indication that their initial faith had not been empty, but that they indeed were chosen by God to be His people. The proof of this choice, as demonstrated by the fruit in their lives, would have been encouraging to Paul, for he knew that nothing, not even intense persecution, could separate God's chosen ones from His love.

Although one could plausibly interpret Paul's comment as saying God had pre-selected them for salvation without disrupting the flow of thought, yet there is nothing in the text to indicate that his words should be interpreted this way. Given that G1586 was never used in Scripture to speak of that type of selection, it is more likely that he was referring to God's selection of the Thessalonians who had believed as His own treasured people.

2 Peter 1

The last occurrence of G1589 is in Peter's second epistle. In this epistle there are a number of solemn warnings against falling away from the faith. We might expect that Peter wrote the epistle as a rebuke to those who had fallen away. However, we can see he did not address the letter to false teachers or to those whom he thought were in danger of becoming false teachers, but "to those who had obtained like precious faith." He wrote to provide them with a reminder of the reliability and authenticity of the word of God and by it, to further establish them in the truth.

Being well aware of the danger of being led away from the faith back into the corruption of the world, he urged them to exercise diligence in their Christian life.

For if these things are yours and abound, you will be neither barren nor unfruitful in the knowledge of our Lord Jesus Christ. For he who lacks these things is shortsighted, even to blindness, and has forgotten that he was cleansed from his old sins. Therefore, brethren, be even more diligent to make your call and **election** sure, for if you do these things you will never stumble; for so an entrance will be supplied to you abundantly into the everlasting kingdom of our Lord and Savior Jesus Christ. (2 Peter 1:8-11)

The exhortation to "make your...election sure" is unquestionably a challenge to interpret, for what can we do to "make sure," or establish, God's choice? It is certain Peter did not mean that their diligence would keep God from questioning the wisdom of His choice. God does not indecisively second-guess Himself. However, if Peter did not write "make your...election sure" from God's perspective, then what did he mean?

Old Testament Example

We may find it helpful to look for an Old Testament story where there was a need to establish the reality of an earlier choice, and see if there are parallels that will help us understand Peter's meaning. We find such a story in the history of Solomon, near the beginning of his reign, after the death of his father, David.

There was no question that David chose Solomon to be king, for he had clearly stated so a number of times (1 Kings 1:13, 17, 30). However, after David's death, Solomon found it was necessary to take certain steps to make his kingdom sure and to remove every doubt about his right to be king of Israel. He was aware that David had experienced a period where his reign faltered, and many Israelites followed after Absalom. To prevent a similar mishap in his reign, Solomon knew he must be diligent.

Therefore, when Adonijah, his older brother, began to take subtle steps to usurp the throne, Solomon found it necessary to have him executed. In addition, he deemed it necessary to execute Adonijah's most powerful supporter, the mighty general Joab. Then Solomon restricted the movements of Shimei, David's most vocal critic, to prevent him from stirring up unrest across the countryside. When Shimei broke his agreement with Solomon and left Jerusalem, he also had him executed. When these things were completed, Scripture says that the kingdom was established in the hand of Solomon (1 Kings 2:46).

In this story, we understand the establishment of the kingdom in Solomon's hand did not mean that he successfully prevented his father from changing his mind, nor that he managed to reassure himself of his selection to the throne. We understand the phrase to mean that he achieved a permanent acceptance of his rule by all those around him.

In the same way, Peter's exhortation, to "make your...election sure," was not a call for them to somehow prevent God from changing His mind, nor for them to find reassurance of their selection for salvation. Instead, we should understand it as a call to achieve, through diligence, a permanent acceptance of their position as the people of God in the sight of all observers.

In the same way that Solomon needed to be diligent to establish his throne and prevent any faltering of his reign, the believers needed to be diligent in order to establish their position as the people of God and avoid any stumbling in their life. According to Peter, any believer who was careless in their life would find themselves barren and unfruitful in the knowledge of Christ. They would inevitably stumble, and raise doubt in the minds of all observers regarding the validity of their claim as the people of God. In such a sad case, although they may have been the elect, they would certainly not be well established in their position.

We see, then, that G1589 evidently referred to God's choice to make them His people.

Before we leave this passage, notice that Peter was writing to people who were at risk of stumbling in their lives. If we were to look at the remainder of his epistle, we would see that there are two distinct groups of people who stumble. There are those who are like a dog returning to his vomit, or like a sow returning to her wallowing. These are individuals who made a choice to follow God but never obtained the precious faith. Peter was not exhorting them, for a mere exhortation is not capable of turning the ungodly from their mire. The second group was those who had obtained the precious faith, but by negligence in their life, they would be in danger of stumbling into the old sins from which they had been cleansed. These people were chosen by God to be His people because they believed.

In his use of G1589, Peter made clear he was exhorting the second group. God had made a deliberate choice of them. Unlike the former group, these people could be turned from mire by a mere exhortation, for they had received great and precious promises through which they could become partakers of the divine nature (2 Peter 1:4).

Conclusion

In each of the four passages, we were able to identify the type of choice as one of the types from our survey of G1586. One passage spoke of God's choice of an individual to service. The other passages spoke of God's choice of certain groups to be His people. Although we did see in some passages that one could conceivably interpret a new type of choice (such as, "chosen for salvation"), we did not see any indication that required, or even implied, such an interpretation. Our conclusion must be that the noun G1589 spoke of a G1586 choice with regards to God's selection of individuals. It either spoke of a choice for service or a choice to take them as His people.

Perhaps we might be inclined to think that God's choice of certain individuals to be His people implies that He also chose them to be saved. However, this does not fit with the prototype of Israel. In the nation of Israel, the essential requirement for an individual to become one of the people of God was to be born into the nation. God made this condition clear when He declared to Abraham that He would "be God to you and your descendants after you" (Gen. 17:7). The same basic requirement applies in this age: for an individual to become one of the people of God, they must be born with the life from above. As God determined that the descendants of Abraham would be His people, so He has determined that those who are in Christ will be His people. Thus, when we read of God choosing certain ones, we should remember that Scripture teaches He chooses the believers to be His people.

~ ~ ~   ~ ~ ~   ~ ~ ~

We have reached the end of our surveys on the words related to election, and have found that Scripture does not indicate that they were used in the sense of individuals pre-selected for salvation. The implications of this are profound. We may now find it useful to re-evaluate our understanding of a number of passages. We may also need to come to an understanding of what it means to be elect. It is evident this was a significant concept in the New Testament, but what was the significance? Perhaps it would be good to take a small peek at what the concept of election meant to the apostles.

10

Doc Election

The Apostle's Doctrine

Greetings. It's a pleasure to meet you. My name is Doctrine Of Election, but you may call me Doc if you wish. The fact that you are here indicates you have persevered through the word studies of G1586 (chose), G1588 (elect), and G1589 (election). I suppose you are to be commended for your tenacity. I trust the studies were helpful in clarifying the scriptural use of those terms? Perhaps there is yet a lingering question of the implications of the surveys in the present context of your life? Maybe you wonder what it actually means to be of the elect in the New Testament sense? If so, then I invite you to take a brief look with me at the Apostle's doctrine regarding the topic. I can assure you that to be one of the elect is to inhabit the best position in all creation.

Generally, when the apostles spoke of the elect, they were referring to believers in the Lord Jesus Christ. However, on occasion, they also referred to the Jews as a group of elect people. This election was distinct from the election of believers. It encompassed the entire nation of Israel, and included both godly and ungodly Jews (see Romans 11:28 for an example of ungodly Jews who were called elect). Although they were distinct types of election, there are a number of similarities between the two. The similarities are so strong that the election of the Israelite nation can serve as a prototype for the spiritual realities in Christ. By looking at the choice of Israel, one can begin to understand the nature of God's choice of the elect in Christ.

> *"For you are a holy people to the Lord your God; the Lord your God has chosen you to be a people for Himself, a special treasure above all the peoples on the face of the earth." (Deuteronomy 7:6)*

Israel was chosen to be God's peculiar treasure, valued above all the nations of the earth. They were not chosen because they possessed inherent characteristics which set them apart from all other nations. Nor were they greater in number, but were instead few; they were not more willing to obey, but were stiff-necked; they were not more willing to follow, but continually went astray. With regards to characteristics and qualities, they were no different than the rest of humanity. Why, then, did God choose them to be His people?

> *The Lord did not set His love on you nor choose you because you were more in number than any other people, for you were the least of all peoples; but because the Lord loves you, and because He would keep the oath which He swore to your fathers, the Lord has brought you out with a mighty hand, and redeemed you from the house of bondage, from the hand of Pharaoh king of Egypt. (Deuteronomy 7:7-8)*

He chose them because He is a God of love, and because they were the children of Abraham, Isaac, and Jacob.

The same applies to the elect in Christ. They were not chosen because they possessed inherent characteristics which set them apart from all other people. They themselves readily confessed that we "once conducted ourselves in the lusts of our flesh, fulfilling the desires of the flesh and of the mind, and were by nature of wrath, just as the others." (Ephesians 2:3). Why, then, did God choose them to be His people? "...because of His great love with which He loved us... made us alive together with Christ..." (Ephesians 2:4-5). Thus, God chose them because He is a God of love, and because in giving them life He made them the children of God. If God chose the nation of Israel as His special treasure because they were the children of Abraham, how much more likely would He be to choose as His special treasure those who are His children? Therefore, we see that the prototype of the nation of Israel first teaches us that the elect in Christ are God's special treasure. We could look for further parallels, but let us leave that for later study and turn to the doctrine of the apostles themselves.

Let us look at Peter's teaching on the topic as recorded in his first epistle. In the second chapter, Peter drew the attention of his readers to the Lord Jesus Christ, reminding them that He was "rejected by men, but chosen (G1588) by God and precious..." (1 Peter 2:4). Although mankind rejected Him, God greatly delighted in Him. You may recall how more than once the voice of God breached the veil of Heaven to express His delight in His beloved Son. There is no question that none have been as greatly beloved or delighted in as the only begotten Son of God. Notice how Peter used the adjective G1588 to concisely convey the pleasure that the Father had in His Son. Then, notice how he later used the same adjective in the description of the believers: "You are a chosen (G1588) generation, a royal priesthood, a holy nation, His own special people... who once were not a people but are now the people of God" (1 Peter 2:9-10). Peter was encouraging these dear, persecuted believers with the reality that God had the same type of delight in them that He had in His Son.

The fundamental truth is the elect are God's special, treasured people. While it is true that God loves the whole world, He especially loves those who are His people. They are treasured and valued as the richest treasure in all creation.

Moving on from Peter's doctrine, let us proceed to Paul's writings. Paul expressed the steadfastness of God's love for the elect in the eighth chapter of his epistle to the Romans. He writes that although the elect had suffered and continue to suffer under immense and terrible trials, yet no level of the world's hatred or catastrophes can dampen Christ's love for the elect. There is no power or living being mighty enough to shake loose the elect from the love of God which is in Christ Jesus our Lord (Romans 8:39).

Turning to Paul's letter to the Ephesians, we see he indicated the immeasurable extent of the love of God for His elect. He wrote of his prayer that the believers would be able to comprehend what is the width and length and depth and height – to know the love of Christ which passes knowledge (Ephesians 3:17-19).

We certainly get the sense from Paul's doctrine that God does not hold back any of His love for the elect. Indeed, it appears that out of all God has created, there is nothing as precious and beloved as His elect.

This, in brief, is the apostle's doctrine regarding the elect. When the term "elect" occurs in the New Testament, it is referring to the group of people whom God has made His own, who are His inheritance, His most precious treasure out of all He has created.

We could continue, perhaps indefinitely, looking at how God views the elect in Christ, but I leave that for your personal exploration and discovery. Hopefully, what I've shared with you thus far will provide a good foundation for you to build upon. God bless.

11

GOD'S CHOICE AND MAN'S RESPONSIBILITY

Putting it All Together

But as many as received Him, to them He gave
the right to become children of God,
to those who believe in His name: who were born,
not of blood, nor of the will of the flesh, nor of the
will of man, but of God.

John 1:12-13

As discussed in earlier chapters, "election" does not refer to God's choice of individuals to receive salvation, but of God's selection of a people for Himself. However, this does not conclusively rule out the possibility of God choosing whom He will save. In fact, the verses above clearly indicate that God does choose who will be born again. According to the text, the new birth does not come through lineage; that is, one is not born into eternal life by having godly parents. Nor does the new birth come from the longing of the individual, regardless of the purity and strength of that desire. Nor can one person pronounce new life upon another. Only God, the source of life, can bring forth new life in a person. He alone determines who will be born again. This truth is clearly proclaimed in the New Testament and must be accepted.

If we can accept that God sovereignly chooses whom He will save, then the question that should naturally follow is, how does God decide whom He will save? Happily, Scripture is not reluctant to give us the answer. Even the passage above alludes to the basis of God's choice. It is the will of the Sovereign God to give life to those who believe in the name of the Lord Jesus.

Although the answer is simple and straightforward, it is not without a level of complexity. Later in his gospel, John shows that not everyone who believed in the name of Jesus was saved. For example, during Passover there "were many [who] believed in His name when they saw the signs which He did. But Jesus did not commit Himself to them..." (John 2:23-24). The phrase, "believed in His name," in this verse is identical to the expression in John 1:12-13 and we might have assumed that God would grant salvation to these people. However, perhaps to our confusion, Verse 24 clearly indicates that Jesus did not receive these people.

Thankfully, John did not leave us in the dark regarding why Jesus didn't commit Himself to these enthusiastic people. In the preceding story, he referenced the faith of Jesus' disciples when they "believed the Scripture and the word which Jesus had said." (John 2:22). In other words, the disciples listened to the word of Jesus and embraced it as truth. John placed the two stories next to each other to provide a stark contrast between the two types of belief. The disciples heard and believed the word of Jesus, but there is no indication that the other people gave the slightest heed to what Jesus said. Evidently, they believed in Him for his miracles, not for the word which He spoke. For that reason, their faith was not accounted to them for righteousness.

Anticipating the possibility of lingering confusion on the differences of faith, John presented additional stories which served as real life illustrations. For example, in Chapter 4, he recorded three stories which demonstrated the characteristics of belief based on the word of the Lord Jesus. The Samaritan woman at the well believed in Him when He stated that He was the Messiah (John 4:26, 29). The Samaritan people of the village believed in Him because they heard for themselves what He said (John 4:42). Finally, the nobleman whose son lay dying at home vividly exhibited what it was to simply take Jesus at His word and to believe what He said (John 4:50). These people displayed the faith which came by hearing the word of God and were received by Jesus.

In Chapter 6, John presented the crowd as an example of those enamored with the Lord's miracles but who rejected His words. When Jesus told them that he was the bread from heaven, they murmured, "Is not this Jesus, the son of Joseph, whose father and mother we know? How is it then that He says, 'I have come down from heaven?'" (John 6:42). They saw the loaves multiplied and believed in the Lord, even to the point where they would pursue him across the sea of Galilee. However, they did not receive His word and so He did not receive them.

To further clarify the point, in Chapter 5 John recorded a conversation between the Lord and the Jews. The Lord declared "the Father judges no one, but has committed all judgment to the Son" (John 5:22). That is, the Father gave the Son the authority to decide who would be granted life and who would be condemned. In the next breath, the Lord plainly indicated whom He would select to receive life. "Most assuredly, I say to you, he who hears My word and believes in Him who sent Me has everlasting life, and shall not come into judgment, but has passed from death into life." (John 5:24). Thus did the Judge of all humankind declare the verdict: life would be given to the person whose faith was based on His word. He would not give life to those who heard but did not believe. Faith was necessary. Nor would He give life to those who had faith in something other than His word. Only those who heard his word and believed would receive life.

Paul also referred to God's deliberate choice, with regards to showing mercy. "I will have mercy on whomever I will have mercy, and I will have compassion on whomever I will have compassion." (Romans 9:15). God declared that He unilaterally makes the decision on whether mercy is shown or not. This statement referenced the time when God chose to show mercy to the stiff-necked children of Israel in the wilderness but did not show mercy to Pharaoh and his Egyptian army. Paul saw that the deliberate choice on that day compared to his current situation where God chose to withdraw His mercy from Israel. In Paul's mind, the reason for the removal was evident, "Israel... has not attained to the law of righteousness. Why? Because they did not seek it by faith, but as it were, by the works of the law." (Romans 9:31-32). God chose not to show mercy to the nation of Israel despite their tireless pursuit after righteousness. Why? Because they did not believe.

Does God choose who will be saved? Indeed He does, but what type of choice is it? Is it a random choice or does it have a basis? Scripture is very clear on this point. God calls to mankind, stretching His hands out to them in invitation. Although they hear, many reject the call. However, there are those who have humble hearts before God, receive His word and believe. We can say with full confidence that God gives eternal life to these. How can we be so confident? For the simple reason that God said it would be so. God has bound Himself to His word, that whosoever believes in Him shall not perish but have eternal life.

We should not get this order mixed up and think that our faith somehow produces eternal life within us. Or that we compel God to save us by the purity and strength of our faith. We need to recognize that God makes a deliberate decision to save certain individuals. We also need to understand that it is not a random choice by God. God has clearly revealed to us His criteria in making the decision to grant an individual eternal life. He looks for faith which is founded on His word.

A

APPENDIX A

G1586

Throughout the New Testament and the LXX, G1586 is generally translated as follows: choose, chose, chosen. It is translated other ways, but these are the most predominate.

The purpose of this appendix is to list each occurrence of this word within the LXX and the New Testament for the convenience of the reader. The verses in which the word is found have been broken up into the following categories:

Chosen by God: People, OT

Chosen by God: People, NT

Chosen by God: Places, OT

Chosen by God: Things

Chosen by Man, OT

Chosen by Man, NT

Other Uses

A couple verses are listed in more than one category due to their content. Some of the verses have a following note in *italics*. These notes are intended to stir the reader's thinking and encourage continued study in this topic.

This listing of verses is intended to be an exhaustive list, but there is the possibility of an omission or two. Please be aware that any omission is unintentional.

Throughout this appendix, **bold italics** will be used to indicate the Greek word of interest within the quoted passage.

~ ~ ~   ~ ~ ~   ~ ~ ~

Chosen By God: People, OT

Numbers 16:5 – and he spoke to Korah and all his company, saying, "Tomorrow morning the LORD will show who is His and who is holy, and will cause him to come near to Him. That one whom He **chooses** He will cause to come near to Him.

Numbers 16:7 – "put fire in them and put incense in them before the LORD tomorrow, and it shall be that the man whom the LORD **chooses** is the holy one. You take too much upon yourselves, you sons of Levi!"

Numbers 17:5 – "And it shall be that the rod of the man whom I **choose** will blossom; thus I will rid Myself of the complaints of the children of Israel, which they make against you."

Deuteronomy 4:37 – "And because He loved your fathers, therefore He **chose** their descendants after them; and He brought you out of Egypt with His Presence, with His mighty power,

Deuteronomy 7:7 – "The LORD did not set His love on you nor **choose** you because you were more in number than any other people, for you were the least of all peoples;

Deuteronomy 10:15 – "The LORD delighted only in your fathers, to love them; and He **chose** their descendants after them, you above all peoples, as it is this day.

Deuteronomy 14:2 – "For you are a holy people to the LORD your God, and the LORD has **chosen** you to be a people for

Himself, a special treasure above all the peoples who are on the face of the earth.

Deuteronomy 17:15 – "you shall surely set a king over you whom the LORD your God **chooses**; one from among your brethren you shall set as king over you; you may not set a foreigner over you, who is not your brother.

Deuteronomy 18:5 – "For the LORD your God has **chosen** him out of all your tribes to stand to minister in the name of the LORD, him and his sons forever.

1 Samuel 2:28 – 'Did I not **choose** him out of all the tribes of Israel to be My priest, to offer upon My altar, to burn incense, and to wear an ephod before Me? And did I not give to the house of your father all the offerings of the children of Israel made by fire?

1 Samuel 10:24 – And Samuel said to all the people, "Do you see him whom the LORD has **chosen**, that there is no one like him among all the people?" So all the people shouted and said, "Long live the king!"

> *As a note of interest, 1 Samuel 12:13 (listed below) states that the people chose Saul as king.*

1 Samuel 16:8-10 – So Jesse called Abinadab, and made him pass before Samuel. And he said, "Neither has the LORD **chosen** this one." Then Jesse made Shammah pass by. And he said, "Neither has the LORD **chosen** this one." Thus Jesse made seven of his sons pass before Samuel. And Samuel said to Jesse, "The LORD has not **chosen** these."

> *A point to consider is why God chose David: it is because He could see in David's heart that he had a heart to serve God. It was the state of David's heart which caused God to choose him. See 1 Kings 11:34 below.*

2 Samuel 6:21 – So David said to Michal, "It was before the LORD, who **chose** me instead of your father and all his house, to

appoint me ruler over the people of the LORD, over Israel. Therefore I will play music before the LORD.

1 Kings 3:8 – "And Your servant is in the midst of Your people whom You have **chosen**, a great people, too numerous to be numbered or counted.

1 Kings 8:16 – 'Since the day that I brought My people Israel out of Egypt, I have **chosen** no city from any tribe of Israel in which to build a house, that My name might be there; but I **chose** David to be over My people Israel.'

1 Kings 11:34 – 'However I will not take the whole kingdom out of his hand, because I have made him ruler all the days of his life for the sake of My servant David, whom I **chose** because he kept My commandments and My statutes.

> *Notice how God chose because of what David did. It was not a choice from random.*

1 Chronicles 15:2 – Then David said, "No one may carry the ark of God but the Levites, for the LORD has **chosen** them to carry the ark of God and to minister before Him forever."

1 Chronicles 28:4-6 – "However the LORD God of Israel **chose** me above all the house of my father to be king over Israel forever, for He has **chosen** Judah to be the ruler. And of the house of Judah, the house of my father, and among the sons of my father, He was pleased with me to make me king over all Israel. "And of all my sons (for the LORD has given me many sons) He has **chosen** my son Solomon to sit on the throne of the kingdom of the LORD over Israel. "Now He said to me, 'It is your son Solomon who shall build My house and My courts; for I have **chosen** him to be My son, and I will be his Father.

2 Chronicles 6:5-6 – 'Since the day that I brought My people out of the land of Egypt, I have **chosen** no city from any tribe of Israel in which to build a house, that My name might be there, nor did I **choose** any man to be a ruler over My people

Israel. 'Yet I have **chosen** Jerusalem, that My name may be there, and I have **chosen** David to be over My people Israel.'

Nehemiah 9:7 – "You are the LORD God, Who **chose** Abram, And brought him out of Ur of the Chaldeans, And gave him the name Abraham;

Psalms 33:12 – Blessed is the nation whose God is the LORD, The people He has **chosen** as His own inheritance.

Psalms 65:4 – Blessed is the man You **choose**, And cause to approach You, That he may dwell in Your courts. We shall be satisfied with the goodness of Your house, Of Your holy temple.

Psalms 78:67-68 – Moreover He rejected the tent of Joseph, And did not **choose** the tribe of Ephraim, but **chose** the tribe of Judah, Mount Zion which He loved.

Psalms 78:70 – He also **chose** David His servant, And took him from the sheepfolds;

Psalms 105:26 – He sent Moses His servant, And Aaron whom He had **chosen**.

Psalms 135:4 – For the LORD has **chosen** Jacob for Himself, Israel for His special treasure.

Isaiah 14:1 – For the LORD will have mercy on Jacob, and will still **choose** Israel, and settle them in their own land. The strangers will be joined with them, and they will cling to the house of Jacob.

Isaiah 41:8-9 – "But you, Israel, are My servant, Jacob whom I have **chosen**, The descendants of Abraham My friend. You whom I have taken from the ends of the earth, And called from its farthest regions, And said to you, 'You are My servant, I have **chosen** you and have not cast you away:

Isaiah 43:10 – "You are My witnesses," says the LORD, "And My servant whom I have **chosen**, That you may know and believe Me, And understand that I am He. Before Me there was no God formed, Nor shall there be after Me.

Isaiah 44:1-2 – "Yet hear now, O Jacob My servant, And Israel whom I have **chosen**. Thus says the LORD who made you And formed you from the womb, who will help you: 'Fear not, O Jacob My servant; And you, Jeshurun, whom I have **chosen**.

Isaiah 49:7 – Thus says the LORD, The Redeemer of Israel, their Holy One, To Him whom man despises, To Him whom the nation abhors, To the Servant of rulers: "Kings shall see and arise, Princes also shall worship, Because of the LORD who is faithful, The Holy One of Israel; And He has **chosen** You."

Jeremiah 33:24 – "Have you not considered what these people have spoken, saying, 'The two families which the LORD has **chosen**, He has also cast them off'? Thus they have despised My people, as if they should no more be a nation before them.

This passage indicates that God's choice is unchanging. He does not go back on His choice.

Ezekiel 20:38 – "I will **purge**[choose] the rebels from among you, and those who transgress against Me; I will bring them out of the country where they dwell, but they shall not enter the land of Israel. Then you will know that I am the LORD.

Chosen By God: People, NT

Mark 13:20 – "And unless the Lord had shortened those days, no flesh would be saved; but for the elect's sake, whom He **chose**, He shortened the days.

Luke 6:13 – And when it was day, He called His disciples to Himself; and from them He **chose** twelve whom He also named apostles:

John 6:70 – Jesus answered them, "Did I not **choose** you, the twelve, and one of you is a devil?"

John 13:18 – "I do not speak concerning all of you. I know whom I have **chosen**; but that the Scripture may be fulfilled, 'He who eats bread with Me has lifted up his heel against Me.'

John 15:16 – "You did not **choose** Me, but I **chose** you and appointed you that you should go and bear fruit, and that your fruit should remain, that whatever you ask the Father in My name He may give you.

John 15:19 – "If you were of the world, the world would love its own. Yet because you are not of the world, but I **chose** you out of the world, therefore the world hates you.

Acts 1:2 – until the day in which He was taken up, after He through the Holy Spirit had given commandments to the apostles whom He had **chosen**,

Acts 1:24 – And they prayed and said, "You, O Lord, who know the hearts of all, show which of these two You have **chosen**

Acts 13:17 – "The God of this people Israel **chose** our fathers, and exalted the people when they dwelt as strangers in the land of Egypt, and with an uplifted arm He brought them out of it.

Acts 15:7 – And when there had been much dispute, Peter rose up and said to them: "Men and brethren, you know that a good while ago God **chose** among us, that by my mouth the Gentiles should hear the word of the gospel and believe.

Ephesians 1:4 – just as He **chose** us in Him before the foundation of the world, that we should be holy and without blame before Him in love,

James 2:5 – Listen, my beloved brethren: Has God not **chosen** the poor of this world to be rich in faith and heirs of the kingdom which He promised to those who love Him?

Chosen By God: Places, OT

Deuteronomy 1:33 – "who went in the way before you to **search** out a place for you to pitch your tents, to show you the way you should go, in the fire by night and in the cloud by day.

Deuteronomy 12:5 – "But you shall seek the place where the LORD your God **chooses**, out of all your tribes, to put His name for His dwelling place; and there you shall go.

Deuteronomy 12:11 – "then there will be the place where the LORD your God **chooses** to make His name abide. There you shall bring all that I command you: your burnt offerings, your sacrifices, your tithes, the heave offerings of your hand, and all your choice offerings which you vow to the LORD.

Deuteronomy 12:14 – "but in the place which the LORD **chooses**, in one of your tribes, there you shall offer your burnt offerings, and there you shall do all that I command you.

Deuteronomy 12:18 – "But you must eat them before the LORD your God in the place which the LORD your God **chooses**, you and your son and your daughter, your male servant and your female servant, and the Levite who is within your gates; and you shall rejoice before the LORD your God in all to which you put your hands.

Deuteronomy 12:21 – "If the place where the LORD your God **chooses** to put His name is too far from you, then you may slaughter from your herd and from your flock which the LORD has given you, just as I have commanded you, and you may eat within your gates as much as your heart desires.

Deuteronomy 12:26 – "Only the holy things which you have, and your vowed offerings, you shall take and go to the place which the LORD **chooses**.

Moses tells them to obey these commands that it may go well with them. They are to go to the place where the Lord chooses instead of wherever they feel like going.

Deuteronomy 14:23-25 – "And you shall eat before the LORD your God, in the place where He **chooses** to make His name abide, the tithe of your grain and your new wine and your oil, of the firstborn of your herds and your flocks, that you may learn to fear the LORD your God always. "But if the journey is too long for you, so that you are not able to carry the tithe, or if the place where the LORD your God **chooses** to put His name is too far from you, when the LORD your God has blessed you, "then you shall exchange it for money, take the money in your hand, and go to the place which the LORD your God **chooses**.

Deuteronomy 15:20 – "You and your household shall eat it before the LORD your God year by year in the place which the LORD **chooses**.

Deuteronomy 16:2 – "Therefore you shall sacrifice the Passover to the LORD your God, from the flock and the herd, in the place where the LORD **chooses** to put His name.

Deuteronomy 16:6-7 – "but at the place where the LORD your God **chooses** to make His name abide, there you shall sacrifice the Passover at twilight, at the going down of the sun, at the time you came out of Egypt. "And you shall roast and eat it in the place which the LORD your God **chooses**, and in the morning you shall turn and go to your tents.

Deuteronomy 16:11 – "You shall rejoice before the LORD your God, you and your son and your daughter, your male servant and your female servant, the Levite who is within your gates, the stranger and the fatherless and the widow who are among you, at the place where the LORD your God **chooses** to make His name abide.

Deuteronomy 16:15-16 – "Seven days you shall keep a sacred feast to the LORD your God in the place which the LORD **chooses**, because the LORD your God will bless you in all your produce and in all the work of your hands, so that you surely rejoice. "Three times a year all your males shall appear before the LORD your God in the place which He **chooses**: at the Feast of Unleavened Bread, at the Feast of Weeks, and at the Feast of Tabernacles; and they shall not appear before the LORD empty-handed.

Deuteronomy 17:8 – "If a matter arises which is too hard for you to judge, between degrees of guilt for bloodshed, between one judgment or another, or between one punishment or another, matters of controversy within your gates, then you shall arise and go up to the place which the LORD your God **chooses**.

Deuteronomy 17:10 – "You shall do according to the sentence which they pronounce upon you in that place which the LORD **chooses**. And you shall be careful to do according to all that they order you.

Deuteronomy 18:6 – "So if a Levite comes from any of your gates, from where he dwells among all Israel, and comes with all the desire of his mind to the place which the LORD **chooses**,

Deuteronomy 26:2 – "that you shall take some of the first of all the produce of the ground, which you shall bring from your land that the LORD your God is giving you, and put it in a basket and go to the place where the LORD your God **chooses** to make His name abide.

Deuteronomy 31:11 – "when all Israel comes to appear before the LORD your God in the place which He **chooses**, you shall read this law before all Israel in their hearing.

Joshua 9:27 – And that day Joshua made them woodcutters and water carriers for the congregation and for the altar of the LORD, in the place which He would **choose**, even to this day.

1 Kings 8:16 – 'Since the day that I brought My people Israel out of Egypt, I have **chosen** no city from any tribe of Israel in which to build a house, that My name might be there; but I **chose** David to be over My people Israel.'

1 Kings 8:44 – "When Your people go out to battle against their enemy, wherever You send them, and when they pray to the LORD toward the city which You have **chosen** and the temple which I have built for Your name,

1 Kings 8:48 – "and when they return to You with all their heart and with all their soul in the land of their enemies who led them away captive, and pray to You toward their land which You gave to their fathers, the city which You have **chosen** and the temple which I have built for Your name:

1 Kings 11:13 – "However I will not tear away the whole kingdom; I will give one tribe to your son for the sake of My servant David, and for the sake of Jerusalem which I have **chosen**."

1 Kings 11:32 – '(but he shall have one tribe for the sake of My servant David, and for the sake of Jerusalem, the city which I have **chosen** out of all the tribes of Israel),

1 Kings 11:36 – 'And to his son I will give one tribe, that My servant David may always have a lamp before Me in Jerusalem, the city which I have **chosen** for Myself, to put My name there.

1 Kings 14:21 – And Rehoboam the son of Solomon reigned in Judah. Rehoboam was forty-one years old when he became king. He reigned seventeen years in Jerusalem, the city which the LORD had **chosen** out of all the tribes of Israel, to put His name there. His mother's name was Naamah, an Ammonitess.

2 Kings 21:7 – He even set a carved image of Asherah that he had made, in the house of which the LORD had said to David and to Solomon his son, "In this house and in Jerusalem, which I have **chosen** out of all the tribes of Israel, I will put My name forever;

2 Kings 23:27 – And the LORD said, "I will also remove Judah from My sight, as I have removed Israel, and will cast off this city Jerusalem which I have **chosen**, and the house of which I said, 'My name shall be there.'"

2 Chronicles 6:5-6 – 'Since the day that I brought My people out of the land of Egypt, I have **chosen** no city from any tribe of Israel in which to build a house, that My name might be there, nor did I **choose** any man to be a ruler over My people

Israel. 'Yet I have **chosen** Jerusalem, that My name may be there, and I have **chosen** David to be over My people Israel.'

2 Chronicles 6:34 – "When Your people go out to battle against their enemies, wherever You send them, and when they pray to You toward this city which You have **chosen** and the temple which I have built for Your name,

2 Chronicles 6:38 – "and when they return to You with all their heart and with all their soul in the land of their captivity, where they have been carried captive, and pray toward their land which You gave to their fathers, the city which You have **chosen**, and toward the temple which I have built for Your name:

2 Chronicles 7:12 – Then the LORD appeared to Solomon by night, and said to him: "I have heard your prayer, and have **chosen** this place for Myself as a house of sacrifice.

2 Chronicles 7:16 – "For now I have **chosen** and sanctified this house, that My name may be there forever; and My eyes and My heart will be there perpetually.

2 Chronicles 12:13 – Thus King Rehoboam strengthened himself in Jerusalem and reigned. Now Rehoboam was forty-one years old when he became king; and he reigned seventeen years in Jerusalem, the city which the LORD had **chosen** out of all the tribes of Israel, to put His name there. His mother's name was Naamah, an Ammonitess.

2 Chronicles 33:7 – He even set a carved image, the idol which he had made, in the house of God, of which God had said to David and to Solomon his son, "In this house and in Jerusalem, which I have **chosen** out of all the tribes of Israel, I will put My name forever;

Nehemiah 1:9 – 'but if you return to Me, and keep My commandments and do them, though some of you were cast out to the farthest part of the heavens, yet I will gather them from there, and bring them to the place which I have **chosen** as a dwelling for My name.'

Psalms 132:13 – For the LORD has **chosen** Zion; He has desired it for His dwelling place:

Zechariah 3:2 – And the LORD said to Satan, "The LORD rebuke you, Satan! The LORD who has **chosen** Jerusalem rebuke you! Is this not a brand plucked from the fire?"

Chosen By God: Things

Psalms 47:4 – He will **choose** our inheritance for us, The excellence of Jacob whom He loves. Selah

Isaiah 58:5-6 – Is it a fast that I have **chosen**, A day for a man to afflict his soul? Is it to bow down his head like a bulrush, And to spread out sackcloth and ashes? Would you call this a fast, And an acceptable day to the LORD? "Is this not the fast that I have **chosen**: To loose the bonds of wickedness, To undo the heavy burdens, To let the oppressed go free, And that you break every yoke?

Isaiah 66:4 – So will I **choose** their delusions, And bring their fears on them; Because, when I called, no one answered, When I spoke they did not hear; But they did evil before My eyes, And **chose** that in which I do not delight."

1Cor 1:27-28 – But God has **chosen** the foolish things of the world to put to shame the wise, and God has **chosen** the weak things of the world to put to shame the things which are mighty; and the base things of the world and the things which are despised God has **chosen**, and the things which are not, to bring to nothing the things that are,

Chosen By Man, OT

Genesis 6:2 – that the sons of God saw the daughters of men, that they were beautiful; and they took wives for themselves of all whom they **chose**.

Genesis 13:11 – Then Lot **chose** for himself all the plain of Jordan, and Lot journeyed east. And they separated from each other.

Deuteronomy 30:19 – "I call heaven and earth as witnesses today against you, that I have set before you life and death, blessing and cursing; therefore **choose** life, that both you and your descendants may live;

Joshua 24:15 – "And if it seems evil to you to serve the LORD, **choose** for yourselves this day whom you will serve, whether the gods which your fathers served that were on the other side of the River, or the gods of the Amorites, in whose land you dwell. But as for me and my house, we will serve the LORD."

Joshua 24:22 – So Joshua said to the people, "You are witnesses against yourselves that you have **chosen** the LORD for yourselves, to serve Him." And they said, "We are witnesses!"

Judges 10:14 – "Go and cry out to the gods which you have **chosen**; let them deliver you in your time of distress."

1 Samuel 8:18 – "And you will cry out in that day because of your king whom you have **chosen** for yourselves, and the LORD will not hear you in that day."

1 Samuel 12:13 – "Now therefore, here is the king whom you have **chosen** and whom you have desired. And take note, the LORD has set a king over you.

> *As a note of interest, 1 Samuel 10:24 (listed above) indicates that the Lord chose Saul as king.*

1 Samuel 13:2 – Saul **chose** for himself three thousand men of Israel. Two thousand were with Saul in Michmash and in the mountains of Bethel, and a thousand were with Jonathan in Gibeah of Benjamin. The rest of the people he sent away, every man to his tent.

1 Samuel 17:8 – Then he stood and cried out to the armies of Israel, and said to them, "Why have you come out to line up

for battle? Am I not a Philistine, and you the servants of Saul? **Choose** a man for yourselves, and let him come down to me.

1 Samuel 17:40 – Then he took his staff in his hand; and he **chose** for himself five smooth stones from the brook, and put them in a shepherd's bag, in a pouch which he had, and his sling was in his hand. And he drew near to the Philistine.

2 Samuel 16:18 – And Hushai said to Absalom, "No, but whom the LORD and this people and all the men of Israel **choose**, his I will be, and with him I will remain.

2 Samuel 24:12-13 – "Go and tell David, 'Thus says the LORD: "I offer you three things; **choose** one of them for yourself, that I may do it to you." ' " So Gad came to David and told him; and he said to him, "Shall seven years of famine come to you in your land? Or shall you flee three months before your enemies, while they pursue you? Or shall there be three days' plague in your land? Now **consider** and see what answer I should take back to Him who sent me."

2 Samuel 24:15 – So the LORD sent a plague upon Israel from the morning till the **appointed** time. From Dan to Beersheba seventy thousand men of the people died.

1 Kings 18:23 – "Therefore let them give us two bulls; and let them **choose** one bull for themselves, cut it in pieces, and lay it on the wood, but put no fire under it; and I will prepare the other bull, and lay it on the wood, but put no fire under it.

1 Kings 18:25 – Now Elijah said to the prophets of Baal, "**Choose** one bull for yourselves and prepare it first, for you are many; and call on the name of your god, but put no fire under it."

1 Chronicles 9:22 – All those **chosen** as gatekeepers were two hundred and twelve. They were recorded by their genealogy, in their villages. David and Samuel the seer had appointed them to their trusted office.

1 Chronicles 16:41 – and with them Heman and Jeduthun and the rest who were **chosen**, who were designated by name,

to give thanks to the LORD, because His mercy endures forever;

1 Chronicles 19:10 – When Joab saw that the battle line was against him before and behind, he **chose** some of Israel's best and put them in battle array against the Syrians.

1 Chronicles 21:10 – "Go and tell David, saying, 'Thus says the LORD: "I offer you three things; **choose** one of them for yourself, that I may do it to you." '"

1 Chronicles 21:11 – So Gad came to David and said to him, "Thus says the LORD: '**Choose** for yourself,

Job 29:25 – I **chose** the way for them, and sat as chief; So I dwelt as a king in the army, As one who comforts mourners.

Job 34:33 – Should He repay it according to your terms, Just because you disavow it? You must **choose**, and not I; Therefore speak what you know.

Psalms 84:10 – For a day in Your courts is better than a thousand. I would **rather** [choose to] be a doorkeeper in the house of my God Than dwell in the tents of wickedness.

Proverbs 24:32 – When I saw it, I considered it well; I looked on it and **received** [chose] instruction:

Isaiah 7:15-16 – "Curds and honey He shall eat, that He may know to refuse the evil and **choose** the good. "For before the Child shall know to refuse the evil and **choose** the good, the land that you dread will be forsaken by both her kings.

Isaiah 40:20 – Whoever is too impoverished for such a contribution **Chooses** a tree that will not rot; He seeks for himself a skillful workman To prepare a carved image that will not totter.

Isaiah 41:24 – Indeed you are nothing, And your work is nothing; He who **chooses** you is an abomination.

Isaiah 44:13 – The craftsman stretches out his rule, He **marks** one out with chalk; He fashions it with a plane, He marks it out with the compass, And makes it like the figure of a man, According to the beauty of a man, that it may remain in the house.

Isaiah 56:4 – For thus says the LORD: "To the eunuchs who keep My Sabbaths, And *choose* what pleases Me, And hold fast My covenant,

Isaiah 65:12 – Therefore I will number you for the sword, And you shall all bow down to the slaughter; Because, when I called, you did not answer; When I spoke, you did not hear, But did evil before My eyes, And *chose* that in which I do not delight."

Isaiah 66:3-4 – "He who kills a bull is as if he slays a man; He who sacrifices a lamb, as if he breaks a dog's neck; He who offers a grain offering, as if he offers swine's blood; He who burns incense, as if he blesses an idol. Just as they have *chosen* their own ways, And their soul delights in their abominations, So will I *choose* their delusions, And bring their fears on them; Because, when I called, no one answered, When I spoke they did not hear; But they did evil before My eyes, And *chose* that in which I do not delight."

Joel 2:16 – Gather the people, Sanctify the congregation, *Assemble* [Choose] the elders, Gather the children and nursing babes; Let the bridegroom go out from his chamber, And the bride from her dressing room.

Chosen By Man, NT

Luke 10:42 – "But one thing is needed, and Mary has *chosen* that good part, which will not be taken away from her."

Luke 14:7 – So He told a parable to those who were invited, when He noted how they *chose* the best places, saying to them:

Acts 6:5 – And the saying pleased the whole multitude. And they *chose* Stephen, a man full of faith and the Holy Spirit, and

Philip, Prochorus, Nicanor, Timon, Parmenas, and Nicolas, a proselyte from Antioch,

Acts 15:22 – Then it pleased the apostles and elders, with the whole church, to send *chosen* men of their own company to Antioch with Paul and Barnabas, namely, Judas who was also named Barsabas, and Silas, leading men among the brethren.

Acts 15:25 – it seemed good to us, being assembled with one accord, to send *chosen* men to you with our beloved Barnabas and Paul,

Other Uses, OT

Daniel 11:35 – "And some of those of understanding shall fall, to refine them, *purify* [choose] them, and make them white, until the time of the end; because it is still for the appointed time.

LXX – And of the ones perceiving shall weaken, to purify them by fire, and to *choose*, and to be uncovered until the time of the end. For it is still for a time.

Daniel 12:10 – "Many shall be *purified* [chosen], made white, and refined, but the wicked shall do wickedly; and none of the wicked shall understand, but the wise shall understand.

B

Appendix B

G1588

Throughout the New Testament and the LXX, G1588 is generally translated as follows: choice, chosen, select, elect. It is translated other ways, but these are the most predominate.

The purpose of this appendix is to list each occurrence of this word within the LXX and the New Testament for the convenience of the reader. The verses in which the word is found have been broken up into the following categories:

OT - Choice by Inherent Qualities

OT - Choice by Honored Status

OT - Chosen to be Choice

NT - Elect People

NT - Elect, not people

For some verses in the Old Testament, the English translation of the Hebrew text is significantly different from the English translation of the LXX. In these cases, the LXX translation is included after the Hebrew translation.

This listing of verses is intended to be an exhaustive list, but there is the possibility of an omission or two. Please be aware that any omission is unintentional.

Throughout this appendix, **bold italics** will be used to indicate the Greek word of interest within the quoted passage.

~ ~ ~   ~ ~ ~   ~ ~ ~

OT - Choice by Inherent Qualities

Genesis 23:6 – "Hear us, my lord: You are a mighty prince among us; bury your dead in the **choicest** of our burial places. None of us will withhold from you his burial place, that you may bury your dead."

Genesis 41:2 – Suddenly there came up out of the river seven cows, fine looking and **fat** [choice]; and they fed in the meadow.

Genesis 41:4 – And the ugly and gaunt cows ate up the seven fine looking and **fat** [choice] cows. So Pharaoh awoke.

Genesis 41:5 – He slept and dreamed a second time; and suddenly seven heads of grain came up on one stalk, **plump** [choice] and good.

Genesis 41:7 – And the seven thin heads devoured the seven **plump** [choice] and full heads. So Pharaoh awoke, and indeed, it was a dream.

Genesis 41:18 – "Suddenly seven cows came up out of the river, fine looking and **fat** [choice]; and they fed in the meadow.

Genesis 41:20 – "And the gaunt and ugly cows ate up the first seven, the **fat** [choice] cows.

Exodus 14:7 – Also, he took six hundred **choice** chariots, and all the chariots of Egypt with captains over every one of them.

Exodus 30:23 – "Also take for yourself **quality** spices–five hundred shekels of liquid myrrh, half as much sweet-smelling cinnamon (two hundred and fifty shekels), two hundred and fifty shekels of sweet-smelling cane,

Deuteronomy 12:11 – "then there will be the place where the LORD your God chooses to make His name abide. There you shall bring all that I command you: your burnt offerings, your sacrifices, your tithes, the heave offerings of your hand, and all your *choice* offerings which you vow to the LORD.

Numbers 11:28 – So Joshua the son of Nun, Moses' assistant, one of his *choice* men, answered and said, "Moses my lord, forbid them!"

Judges 20:16 – Among all this people were seven hundred *select* men who were left-handed; every one could sling a stone at a hair's breadth and not miss.

Judges 20:34 And ten thousand *select* men from all Israel came against Gibeah, and the battle was fierce. But the Benjamites did not know that disaster was upon them.

1 Samuel 24:2 – Then Saul took three thousand *chosen* men from all Israel, and went to seek David and his men on the Rocks of the Wild Goats.

1 Samuel 26:2 – Then Saul arose and went down to the Wilderness of Ziph, having three thousand *chosen* men of Israel with him, to seek David in the Wilderness of Ziph.

2 Samuel 8:8 – Also from Betah and from Berothai, cities of Hadadezer, King David took a large amount of bronze.

LXX – And from Betah, and from the **chosen** cities of Hadadezer, king David took exceedingly much brass.

2 Samuel 22:27 – With the *pure* You will show Yourself *pure*; And with the devious You will show Yourself shrewd.

1 Kings 4:23 – ten *fatted* oxen, twenty oxen from the pastures, and one hundred sheep, besides deer, gazelles, roebucks, and fatted fowl.

2 Kings 3:19 – "Also you shall attack every fortified city and every *choice* city, and shall cut down every good tree, and stop up every spring of water, and ruin every good piece of land with stones."

2 Kings 8:12 – And Hazael said, "Why is my lord weeping?" He answered, "Because I know the evil that you will do to the

children of Israel: Their strongholds you will set on fire, and their **young** men you will kill with the sword; and you will dash their children, and rip open their women with child."

2 Kings 19:23 – By your messengers you have reproached the Lord, and said: "By the multitude of my chariots I have come up to the height of the mountains, to the limits of Lebanon; I will cut down its tall cedars and its **choice** cypress trees; I will enter the extremity of its borders, to its fruitful forest.

1 Chronicles 7:40 – All these were the children of Asher, heads of their fathers' houses, **choice** men, mighty men of valor, chief leaders. And they were recorded by genealogies among the army fit for battle; their number was twenty-six thousand.

1 Chronicles 18:8 – Also from Tibhath and from **Chun**, cities of Hadadezer, David brought a large amount of bronze, with which Solomon made the bronze Sea, the pillars, and the articles of bronze.

2 Chronicles 13:3 – Abijah set the battle in order with an army of valiant warriors, four hundred thousand **choice** men. Jeroboam also drew up in battle formation against him with eight hundred thousand **choice** men, mighty men of valor.

Ezra 5:8 – Let it be known to the king that we went into the province of Judea, to the temple of the great God, which is being built with **heavy** [choice] stones, and timber is being laid in the walls; and this work goes on diligently and prospers in their hands.

Nehemiah 5:18 – Now that which was prepared daily was one ox and six **choice** sheep. Also fowl were prepared for me, and once every ten days an abundance of all kinds of wine. Yet in spite of this I did not demand the governor's provisions, because the bondage was heavy on this people.

Job 37:11 – Also with moisture He saturates the thick clouds; He scatters His bright clouds.

LXX - And if a **chosen** cloud plasters over, then his light disperses the cloud,

Psalms 18:26 – With the **pure** You will show Yourself **pure**; And with the devious You will show Yourself shrewd.

Psalms 78:31 – The wrath of God came against them, And slew the stoutest of them, And struck down the **choice** men of Israel.

Psalms 141:4 – Do not incline my heart to any evil thing, To practice wicked works with men who work iniquity; And do not let me eat of their delicacies.

LXX - You should not turn aside my heart to words of wickedness, to make excuses for sins with men working lawlessness; and in no way shall I associate myself with their **choice** ones.

Proverbs 12:24 – The hand of the **diligent** will rule, But the lazy man will be put to forced labor.

Proverbs 8:19 – My fruit is better than gold, yes, than fine gold, And my revenue than **choice** silver.

Proverbs 17:3 – The refining pot is for silver and the furnace for gold, But the LORD tests the hearts.

LXX - As silver and gold tried in a furnace; so **choice** hearts by the Lord.

Song of Solomon 5:15 – His legs are pillars of marble set on bases of fine gold. His countenance is like Lebanon, **excellent** as the cedars.

Song of Solomon 6:9 – My dove, my perfect one, Is the only one, the only one of her mother, the **favorite** of the one who bore her. The daughters saw her and called her blessed, the queens and the concubines, and they praised her.

Song of Solomon 6:10 – Who is she who looks forth as the morning, fair as the moon, clear as the sun, awesome as an army with banners?

LXX - Who is she, the one looking out as the dawn, fair as the moon, **choice** as the sun, the consternation as troops being set in order.

Isaiah 22:7 – It shall come to pass that your **choicest** valleys shall be full of chariots, and the horsemen shall set themselves in array at the gate.

Isaiah 22:8 – He removed the protection of Judah. You looked in that day to the armor of the House of the Forest;

LXX - And they shall uncover the gates of Judah, and they shall look in that day unto the **choice** houses of the city.

Isaiah 40:30 – Even the youths shall faint and be weary, And the **young** men shall utterly fall,

Isaiah 28:16 – Therefore thus says the Lord GOD: "Behold, I lay in Zion a stone for a foundation, A tried stone, a **precious** cornerstone, a sure foundation; Whoever believes will not act hastily.

Isaiah 42:1 – "Behold! My Servant whom I uphold, My **Elect** One in whom My soul delights! I have put My Spirit upon Him; He will bring forth justice to the Gentiles.

Isaiah 49:2 – And He has made My mouth like a sharp sword; in the shadow of His hand He has hidden Me, and made Me a polished shaft; in His quiver He has hidden Me."

LXX - And he made my mouth as a sharp sword, and under the protection of his hand he hid me. He made me as a **chosen** arrow; and in his quiver he hid me.

Isaiah 54:12 – I will make your pinnacles of rubies, your gates of crystal, and all your walls of **precious** stones.

Jeremiah 3:19 – "But I said: 'How can I put you among the children and give you a pleasant land, a beautiful heritage of the hosts of nations?' "And I said: 'You shall call Me, "My Father," and not turn away from Me.'

LXX - And I said, May it be, O LORD, for You said, I shall arrange you among children, and I shall give to you a **choice** land (the inheritance of God almighty) of nations. And I said, you shall call Me father; and you shall not be turned from me.

Jeremiah 10:17 – Gather up your wares from the land, O inhabitant of the fortress!

LXX - He gathered his support from outside dwelling in **choice** vessels.

Jeremiah 22:7 – I will prepare destroyers against you, everyone with his weapons; they shall cut down your **choice** cedars and cast them into the fire.

Jeremiah 25:34 – "Wail, shepherds, and cry! Roll about in the ashes, you leaders of the flock! For the days of your slaughter and your dispersions are fulfilled; you shall fall like a **precious** vessel.

Jeremiah 31:39 – "The surveyor's line shall again extend straight forward over the hill Gareb; then it shall turn toward Goath.

LXX - And its measurement shall go forth before it unto the hills of Gareb; and it shall be surrounded round about of **choice** stones,

Jeremiah 46:15 – Why are your **valiant** men swept away? They did not stand because the LORD drove them away.

Jeremiah 48:15 – Moab is plundered and gone up from her cities; her **chosen** young men have gone down to the slaughter," says the King, whose name is the LORD of hosts.

Lamentations 1:15 – "The Lord has trampled underfoot all my mighty men in my midst; He has called an assembly against me to crush my **young** men; the Lord trampled as in a winepress the virgin daughter of Judah.

Lamentations 5:13-14 – **Young** men ground at the millstones; boys staggered under loads of wood. The elders have ceased gathering at the gate, and the **young** men from their music.

Ezekiel 7:20 – 'As for the beauty of his ornaments, He set it in majesty; but they made from it the images of their abominations– their detestable things; therefore I have made it like refuse to them.

LXX - A **choice** ornament for pride -- they made them; and images of their abominations they made from them. Because of this I have given them to them for uncleanness.

Ezekiel 19:12 – But she was plucked up in fury, she was cast down to the ground, and the east wind dried her fruit.

Her **strong** branches were broken and withered; the fire consumed them.

Ezekiel 19:14 – Fire has come out from a rod of her branches and devoured her fruit, so that she has no strong branch– a scepter for ruling.' " This is a lamentation, and has become a lamentation.

LXX - And fire came forth from out of a rod of her **choice** ones and devoured her; and a rod of strength was not in her. She is a tribe for a parable of lamentation, and will be for a lamentation.

Ezekiel 25:9 – "therefore, behold, I will clear the territory of Moab of cities, of the cities on its frontier, the glory of the country, Beth Jeshimoth, Baal Meon, and Kirjathaim.

LXX - On account of this, behold, I will disable the shoulder of Moab from the cities of his extremities, the **choice** land, the house of Beth-jeshimoth above the spring of the city by the sea.

Ezekiel 27:20 – "Dedan was your merchant in saddlecloths for riding.

LXX - Dedan were your merchants with **choice** animals for chariots.

Ezekiel 27:24 – "These were your merchants in **choice** items– in purple clothes, in embroidered garments, in chests of multicolored apparel, in sturdy woven cords, which were in your marketplace.

Ezekiel 31:16 – 'I made the nations shake at the sound of its fall, when I cast it down to hell together with those who descend into the Pit; and all the trees of Eden, the **choice** and best of Lebanon, all that drink water, were comforted in the depths of the earth.

Daniel 11:15 – "So the king of the North shall come and build a siege mound, and take a fortified city; and the forces of the South shall not withstand him. Even his **choice** troops shall have no strength to resist.

Amos 5:11 – Therefore, because you tread down the poor and take grain taxes from him, though you have built houses of hewn stone, yet you shall not dwell in them; you have planted pleasant vineyards, but you shall not drink wine from them.

LXX - On account of this, because they struck the poor with their fist, and they took *choice* gifts from them; seeing that you built planed houses, that in no way shall you dwell in them; you planted desirable vineyards, but in no way should you drink of their wine.

Habakkuk 1:16 – Therefore they sacrifice to their net, and burn incense to their dragnet; because by them their share is sumptuous and their food plentiful.

LXX - Because of this he will sacrifice to his dragnet, and burn incense to his casting-net; for by them he fattened his portion, even his *choice* foods.

Zechariah 7:14 – "But I scattered them with a whirlwind among all the nations which they had not known. Thus the land became desolate after them, so that no one passed through or returned; for they made the *pleasant* land desolate."

Zechariah 11:16 – "For indeed I will raise up a shepherd in the land who will not care for those who are cut off, nor seek the young, nor heal those that are broken, nor feed those that still stand. But he will eat the flesh of the *fat* and tear their hooves in pieces.

OT - Choice by Honored Status

2 Samuel 21:6 – "let seven men of his descendants be delivered to us, and we will hang them before the LORD in Gibeah of Saul, whom the LORD *chose*." And the king said, "I will give them."

Psalms 89:19 – Then You spoke in a vision to Your holy one, and said: "I have given help to one who is mighty; I have exalted one **chosen** from the people.

Psalms 106:23 – Therefore He said that He would destroy them, had not Moses His **chosen** one stood before Him in the breach, to turn away His wrath, lest He destroy them.

Haggai 2:7 – 'and I will shake all nations, and they shall come to the Desire of All Nations, and I will fill this temple with glory,' says the LORD of hosts.

LXX - And I shall shake all the nations. And the **chosen** of all the nations shall come, and I will fill this house with glory, says the Lord almighty.

OT - Chosen to be Choice

1 Chronicles 16:13 – O seed of Israel His servant, you children of Jacob, His **chosen** ones!

Psalms 89:3 – "I have made a covenant with My **chosen**, I have sworn to My servant David:

Psalms 105:6 – O seed of Abraham His servant, you children of Jacob, His **chosen** ones!

Psalms 105:43 – He brought out His people with joy, His **chosen** ones with gladness.

Psalms 106:5 – That I may see the benefit of Your **chosen** ones, that I may rejoice in the gladness of Your nation, that I may glory with Your inheritance.

Isaiah 43:20 – The beast of the field will honor Me, the jackals and the ostriches, because I give waters in the wilderness and rivers in the desert, to give drink to My people, My **chosen**.

Isaiah 45:4 – For Jacob My servant's sake, and Israel My **elect**, I have even called you by your name; I have named you, though you have not known Me.

Isaiah 65:9 – I will bring forth descendants from Jacob, and from Judah an heir of My mountains; My *elect* shall inherit it, And My servants shall dwell there.

Isaiah 65:15 – You shall leave your name as a curse to My *chosen*; for the Lord GOD will slay you, and call His servants by another name;

Isaiah 65:22 – They shall not build and another inhabit; they shall not plant and another eat; for as the days of a tree, so shall be the days of My people, and My *elect* shall long enjoy the work of their hands.

NT - Elect People

Matthew 20:16 – "So the last will be first, and the first last. For many are called, but few *chosen*."

> The last sentence of this verse is not contained in some manuscripts

Matthew 22:14 – "For many are called, but few are *chosen*."

Matthew 24:22 – "And unless those days were shortened, no flesh would be saved; but for the *elect's* sake those days will be shortened.

Matthew 24:24 – "For false christs and false prophets will rise and show great signs and wonders to deceive, if possible, even the *elect*.

Matthew 24:31 – "And He will send His angels with a great sound of a trumpet, and they will gather together His *elect* from the four winds, from one end of heaven to the other.

Mark 13:20 – "And unless the Lord had shortened those days, no flesh would be saved; but for the *elect's* sake, whom He chose, He shortened the days.

Mark 13:22 – "For false christs and false prophets will rise and show signs and wonders to deceive, if possible, even the **elect**.

Mark 13:27 – "And then He will send His angels, and gather together His **elect** from the four winds, from the farthest part of earth to the farthest part of heaven.

Luke 18:7 – "And shall God not avenge His own **elect** who cry out day and night to Him, though He bears long with them?

Romans 8:33 – Who shall bring a charge against God's **elect**? It is God who justifies.

Romans 16:13 – Greet Rufus, **chosen** in the Lord, and his mother and mine.

Colossians 3:12 – Therefore, as the **elect** of God, holy and beloved, put on tender mercies, kindness, humility, meekness, longsuffering;

2 Timothy 2:10 – Therefore I endure all things for the sake of the **elect**, that they also may obtain the salvation which is in Christ Jesus with eternal glory.

Titus 1:1 – Paul, a bondservant of God and an apostle of Jesus Christ, according to the faith of God's **elect** and the acknowledgment of the truth which accords with godliness,

1 Peter 1:2 – **Elect** according to the foreknowledge of God the Father, through sanctification of the Spirit, unto obedience and sprinkling of the blood of Jesus Christ: Grace unto you, and peace, be multiplied.

1 Peter 2:9 – But you are a **chosen** generation, a royal priesthood, a holy nation, His own special people, that you may proclaim the praises of Him who called you out of darkness into His marvelous light;

2 John 1:1 – The Elder, To the **elect** lady and her children, whom I love in truth, and not only I, but also all those who have known the truth,

2 John 1:13 – The children of your **elect** sister greet you. Amen.

Revelation 17:14 – "These will make war with the Lamb, and the Lamb will overcome them, for He is Lord of lords and King of kings; and those who are with Him are called, **chosen**, and faithful."

NT - Elect, not people

Note: It is not the author's intent to imply that Jesus was not human; it is merely the author's inability to come up with a satisfactory, succinct, and accurate title for the section. Please accept my apologies.

Luke 23:35 – And the people stood looking on. But even the rulers with them sneered, saying, "He saved others; let Him save Himself if He is the Christ, the **chosen** of God."

1 Timothy 5:21 – I charge you before God and the Lord Jesus Christ and the **elect** angels that you observe these things without prejudice, doing nothing with partiality.

1 Peter 2:4 – Coming to Him as to a living stone, rejected indeed by men, but **chosen** by God and precious,

1 Peter 2:6 – Therefore it is also contained in the Scripture, "Behold, I lay in Zion A chief cornerstone, **elect**, precious, And he who believes on Him will by no means be put to shame."